WARREN HARDING: He had matinee-idol looks and was the first president to invite real Hollywood stars to Washington. But his wife, Florence, managed his political career from start to finish.

ALICE GLASS: A wealthy socialite, she not only went to bed with Lyndon Johnson for almost thirty years, she also taught him table manners.

WILBUR MILLS: He drank as much as two fifths of vodka a day and was completely plastered during most of his brief campaign for the White House in 1972.

Praise for Bill Thomas's Previous Book
CLUB FED

"With a razor-sharp wit and an insider's view of how the capital works, Thomas has written a book that should embarrass every Washington politico. . . . The book is painfully funny—with emphasis on 'painfully.' "
—Tom Powers, *Flint Journal* (MI)

"A sprawling, ribald collection of anecdotes and salacious scandal . . . provide[s] plenty of evidence that Congress richly deserves its reputation."
—Jonathan S. Shapiro, *American Lawyer*

ARTHUR BROWN: Elected to the Senate in 1896, he was the only member of Congress ever to be killed by a jealous mistress.

AMBASSADOR JOSEPH P. KENNEDY: His longtime love affair with actress Gloria Swanson—often conducted in public—provided his sons with an at-home, how-to course in marital infidelity.

BARNEY FRANK: Frank and his love interest Herb Moses made history as the first male couple to dance at the White House.

More Praise for Bill Thomas's
CLUB FED

"Thomas regales readers with a series of familiar malfeasances from the past few years with the only solace that's left: humor."

—*Booklist*

"Thomas presciently illuminates the institutional changes Congress must face regardless of which party is in power."

—David Dahl, *St. Petersburg Times*

REPRESENTATIVE CHARLES WILSON: He only hires ex–beauty queens to work in his Capitol Hill office.

JAMES BATES: One of the worst bosses on Capitol Hill, the representative once attached himself to a female staffer's leg, while they discussed a piece of legislation.

MARION BARRY: After his cocaine conviction, the Washington mayor said "the God force" entered his life in prison, where authorities say he also received oral sex from a female visitor.

More Praise for Bill Thomas's
CLUB FED

Other Books by Bill Thomas

*Club Fed: Power, Money, Sex and Violence
  on Capitol Hill*
Red Tape: Adventure Capitalism in the New Russia
  (with Charles Sutherland)
Lawyers and Thieves (with Roy Grutman)

CAPITAL CONFIDENTIAL

One Hundred Years of Sex, Scandal, and Secrets in Washington, D.C.

BILL THOMAS

Foreword by Ronald Kessler

POCKET BOOKS
New York London Toronto Sydney Tokyo Singapore

An *Original* Publication of POCKET BOOKS

 POCKET BOOKS, a division of Simon & Schuster Inc.
1230 Avenue of the Americas, New York, NY 10020

Thomas, Bill, 1943–
    Capital confidential : one hundred years of sex, scandal, and secrets in
Washington, D.C. / by Bill Thomas ; foreword by Ronald Kessler.
    p.   cm.
    ISBN: 0-671-55310-0
    1. Scandals—Washington (D.C.)—History.   2. Washington (D.C.)—
Social life and customs.   3. Politicians—Washington (D.C.)—
Conduct of life—History.   I. Title.
    F199.T53   1996
    975.3—dc20   95-43121
                                                                          CIP

First Pocket Books trade paperback printing April 1996

10   9   8   7   6   5   4   3   2   1

Cover design by Steven Ferlauto
Front cover photos: top, The National Archives, Nixon Project; bottom,
left to right, UPI/Bettmann, UPI/Bettmann Newsphotos, Reuters/Bettmann,
Reuters/Bettman
Back cover photos: UPI/Bettmann

Printed in the U.S.A.

Contents

Foreword

By Ronald Kessler

It's become fashionable to say that criticism of public officials has gone too far: If the trend continues, no one will want to run for office because no one can meet the impossible standards.

The truth is just the opposite. With some exceptions, the media and the public have become too tolerant of public officials' improprieties. In years past, public officials were said to be held to a higher standard than the rest of the public. No more. Now the criterion for whether an official is fit to hold office is often whether he or she has not been convicted of criminal violations in a court of law.

That was the standard many newspapers suggested be used in determining whether Sen. John Tower should be confirmed as secretary of defense. In its background investigation, the FBI had uncovered extensive evidence of excessive drinking. Such reports would be enough to deny anyone a security clearance. Yet some newspapers dismissed the reports. Instead of expressing outrage that President Bush had submitted the nomination in the first place, the papers questioned the veracity of the reports and pointed out that the allegations against Senator Tower had not been proven in a court of law. But that is not the standard to which nominees for high office should be held. There is no inalienable right to be a cabinet officer. One does not have to be convicted of a crime or be a certifiable mental case to be deemed unfit to serve. The standard should be that behavior that creates questions about the nominee's judgment or integrity should be enough to disqualify him. As Sen. Sam Nunn said at the time, if a man is unfit to serve aboard a Trident missile submarine, he should not be named its ultimate commander.

The Senate rejected the Tower nomination. But it confirmed as a federal judge Robert F. Collins, a New Orleans magistrate, even though the FBI reported that, when a local judge, Collins had traded the services of prostitutes for favorable court decisions. As in the Tower case, many senators ignored the evidence. They said Collins had not been charged with any crime, much less convicted. Yet, as Maximilien Robespierre, the French politician, said, "No man can climb out beyond the limitations of his own character." Sure enough, after he became a federal judge, the FBI received more allegations that Collins was corrupt. As a result of the FBI investigation, Collins was sentenced to six years and ten months in prison for taking a bribe of $100,000 from a convicted marijuana smuggler.

Too often, the electorate exhibits the same kind of amnesia. The fact that Newt Gingrich divorced his wife when she had cancer, then refused to pay sufficient child support, should have been enough reason not to vote for him for dogcatcher, let alone for Congress. In choosing a friend or promoting an employee, one would never select someone with such a background of demonstrated ruthlessness. Yet Gingrich has been talked about as a presidential candidate.

Foreword

In voting for Gingrich, residents of Georgia had to willfully ignore the conflict between Gingrich's behavior toward his own family and his self-proclaimed promise to restore "moral values." Instead, they chose to believe the fairy tale they saw on television—his amiability and campaign promises.

Just as ethical lapses represented by Nixon's "Checkers" speech led inexorably to Watergate, negative character traits such as Gingrich's would be magnified were he to reside at the White House. In the same vein, Clinton's compulsive philandering while governor of Arkansas suggested immaturity, insincerity, poor judgment, and arrogance, which can be seen in the immaturity of the staff he selected and his own indecisiveness and lack of convictions and values.

If voters have come to ignore track records, they also have come to expect and accept hypocrisy. Candidates for president are expected to lie, breaking their campaign promises as soon as they get in the White House. It has become almost a sign that a candidate is *not* presidential if he tells the truth.

At the same time, the press has become less aggressive in undertaking the kind of tedious, costly investigative reporting that uncovers abuse. Since Watergate, the change in the perceived importance of the press has meant the White House and other centers of power try to woo the media even more than before. That coziness, along with the intimidating effect of an increase in libel suits, has led to the virtual disappearance of investigative reporting of any kind at most major newspapers.

Eugene L. Roberts Jr., now managing editor of the *New York Times*, related what happened when he tried to help a student from Japan study investigative reporting in the United States. Except at a handful of papers, the student "found it difficult to find reporters who were spending time on projects," Roberts said. "Some investigative reporters had been reassigned. Some were leaving journalism. Still others were retiring. All gave the same reason. Their newspapers had lost interest in in-depth reporting."

When it does its job, the press is often denounced as irresponsible. As the press has reported each move by the Whitewater independent counsel or the latest gaffes by Clinton's staff, the Clinton White House has claimed the media are engaging in mean-spirited "cannibalism." From Tonya Harding to Michael Jackson, the propagandists of celebrities have criticized the press for going too far in revealing scandal, only to fall silent as the charges initially reported in the media proved to be tamer than the truth. Yet the criticism, particularly when it comes from the White House, can be intimidating.

The problem, then, is not that standards in judging politicians are too high but rather that they are too low. As a result of litigation and legislation, ethical standards in the rest of society have become tighter. In the political arena, little has changed. But if Washington scandals are not new, they are as relevant as today's headlines. For only by understanding the past will Americans learn how to select politicians who will not abuse the public trust in the future.

That is the lesson of Bill Thomas's incisive, comprehensive, and entertaining book.

Richard Nixon, whose name became synonymous with political scandal, is shown here in 1966, practicing his famous "I'm-not-a-crook" gesture. *[Roll Call]*

CAPITAL CONFIDENTIAL

Introduction

Not all Washington wrongdoing is that bad. A lot of the time, in fact, it's not even *wrong*. That's because in the nation's capital, scandal and sleaze are in the eye of the voter. Conduct repulsive enough to cause the loss of an election in one part of the country can have an equal and opposite effect, or none at all, someplace else.

Consider the House banking scandal a few years ago in which over a hundred members of Congress wrote millions of dollars in bounced checks. While some lawmakers involved begged forgiveness, Rep. Charles Wilson, among the worst offenders with eighty-one checks bounced, proudly proclaimed that folks down in Texas *expected* him to get in trouble.

Apparently, he was right. A year later, Texas voters in Wilson's district sent him back to Congress for an eleventh term and presumably more of the same.

Part of the fun of politics is waiting for politicians to misbehave. But that's also part of the difficulty. The current definition of political misbehavior depends on such a wide range of complex variables that the whole concept can change from one elected official to the next.

That's what happened in 1983, when two House members, Dan Crane and Gerry Studds, were both caught having sex with Capitol pages, those bright, idealistic teenage messengers hired to run errands around the Hill. The difference was that Crane had sex with a girl, and Studds had sex with a boy. Voters in Crane's Illinois district were incensed, and he was forced to resign in shame. But Studds's Massachusetts constituents saw nothing to get that upset about, and he's been in office ever since.

As the outrageous has become ordinary, not only is it harder to identify political scandals, but the growing popularity of plea bargains, drug rehab, and other evasive maneuvers has actually made most of them seem like business as usual.

Despite laxer standards, the 1990s could go down as the sleaziest decade Washington has seen in a long time. Some of the juicier accusations have involved the Keating Five (influence peddling), Whitewater (possible campaign fraud), the House banking scam (see above), Rep. Barney Frank (employing a male prostitute), Rep. Donald "Buz" Lukens (contributing to the delinquency of a female minor), Supreme Court Justice Clarence Thomas and Sen. Robert Packwood (unwanted sexual advances), Rep. Mel Reynolds (child pornography), and Rep. Dan Rostenkowski (kickbacks and witness tampering). Five members of Congress have gone to jail (for bribery, racketeering, and tax evasion), and the president was sued for sexual misconduct. However, Bill Clinton, who allegedly ordered a female state employee to kiss his penis when he was governor of Arkansas, may have a valid excuse. According to a witness familiar with the case, Clinton once informed him "he had researched the subject in the Bible and oral sex isn't considered adultery."

For sheer bad taste is there anything to top House Speaker Newt Gingrich, divorcing his first wife while she was in the hospital recovering from a cancer operation? As a matter of fact there is. How about the late Senate chaplain, Rev. Richard Halverson, who once opened a session of that august body with the following prayer:

"Sovereign Lord . . . we pray for the senators running for reelection. . . . Give wisdom to those who direct their campaigns. Give the senators special persuasion in speech . . . and provide wherever needed adequate campaign funds."

This book is a one-hundred-year history of government *in flagrante.* It is about what elected officials, journalists, and other prominent Washingtonians do behind closed doors—and more and more right out in the open. As for the politicians, the raw numbers tell part of the story. Since 1900, thirty-six senators and congressmen have gone to prison. This compares with a grand total of *one* legislative-branch jailbird during all the previous years of the Republic. The 1990s have seen six lawmakers sent up the river. So far, the decade has produced an average of one congressional convict annually. These days, when people on Capitol Hill talk about term limits, you have to wonder if they mean time spent in office or time behind bars.

What is it about winning an election that turns ordinary guys in mustard-colored suits and matching loafers into venal, sex-crazed congressmen? Having more pull and prestige than most of them ever dreamed of probably has a lot to do with it, as evidenced by the fact that the phenomenon has basically the same effect on women. Let's not forget former Rep. Mary Rose Oakar from Ohio, who kept a close companion on her House payroll two years after the woman in question moved to New York.

It's sometimes called "Potomac Fever," an inflation of the ego that seems to affect everyone who thinks that he or she is important enough to be called a Washington insider. The symptoms are vanity, greed, and a firm belief that rules and regulations imposed everywhere else in America don't apply here.

Scandal, needless to say, can occur wherever there are politicians, and since Washington is crawling with them, who knows when the next Warren G. Harding or John F. Kennedy will appear?

"Follow me around. I don't care," said Gary Hart in what had to be the most self-defeating invitation ever made by a presidential candidate. Shortly afterward, reporters who accepted the challenge found Hart shacked up with a blond model while his wife was out of town. Thanks to ever-vigilant media, the lag time between transgression and exposure has been shortened from months, sometimes years, to minutes.

It isn't political power that corrupts, it's all of the temptations that come with it, and no place in America offers more temptation to the temporarily powerful than Washington, D.C.

Given the many candidates to choose from, it wasn't easy picking ones whose misdeeds show how rotten politicians and their friends and associates can really be. Proven malfeasance and prolonged moral turpitude were obviously considerations. Yet the deciding factor wasn't just the abuse of public trust but an accompanying flair for public shamelessness that separates the rank-and-file amateurs from the superstars.

In this year of the century's last presidential election, it's time to take stock of our lapsed leaders, to try to understand their various failings and in the process ask ourselves these two important questions: Why do we keep voting for such incredible slimebags? And what would we do for entertainment without them?

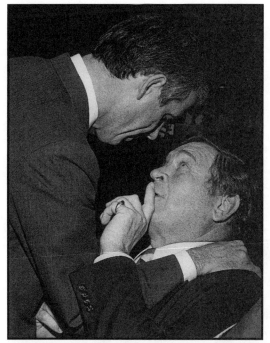

Tony Coelho (left), who quit his House seat after a junk-bond exposé, consoles former Rep. Dan Rostenkowski, indicted on multiple counts of witness tampering and misusing government funds. *[Roll Call]*

Rep. Barney Frank and ex-colleague Mary Rose Oakar dance their troubles away. Frank got caught employing a male prostitute. Oakar was nabbed in the House banking scam. *[Roll Call]*

Two of the Senate's most infamous ladies' men, Ted Kennedy and recent retiree Robert Packwood, compare notes at a women's rights meeting. *[Roll Call]*

After a messy divorce and a confession that he smoked marijuana, House Speaker Newt Gingrich, here with second wife, Marianne, isn't about to let charges of financial misconduct spoil his fun. *[Roll Call]*

1

Unsafe Sex

As the only member of Congress ever to be killed by a jealous mistress, Arthur Brown of Utah deserves a special place among Senate alumni. He may have had a brief career on Capitol Hill, but as a ladies' man no lawmaker ever paid a higher price.

Brown was an ambitious Republican lawyer in Salt Lake City when the state legislature elected him to serve his one and only Senate term in 1896. And he was on his second marriage when, not long afterward, he began his fatal pursuit of Mrs. Anne Bradley, the beautiful wife of a Salt Lake railroad official.

"He was a strange man," Mrs. Bradley said later in court. "He [came] to my house at very unseemly hours, and when I told him it must stop, he answered, 'Darling, we will go through life together. I want you to have a son.'"

When the two were arrested for adultery in 1901, Mrs. Bradley, twenty-eight, had received hundreds of love letters from her persistent admirer, then nearly twice her age. She also had a son she claimed to be his, although at the time she was still living with her husband, who must have wondered why his wife insisted on naming the child Arthur Brown Bradley.

Brown's wife, Isabel, who knew all about the affair, refused to give him a divorce, according to a newspaper report, because "she intended to be presented at court in England . . . and divorced women are restricted." Not to mention husbands with police records.

Following a second arrest on adultery charges, a temporarily reformed Brown promised his wife he would stop seeing Mrs. Bradley and hired a lawyer, Soren X. Christensen, to keep him away from her. Brown and his wife offered Mrs. Bradley a house and $100 a month to leave them alone. But now in full pursuit of the man she loved, she rejected any financial settlement, saying she wanted "nothing but the senator."

Mormon Salt Lake was scandalized. The only consolation, as some residents saw it, was that Brown was a Methodist and Mrs. Bradley a Unitarian.

Unable to stay out of trouble, Brown soon gave his minder the slip, and he and Mrs. Bradley were at it again. This time, they ran off to a resort hotel in Pocatello, Idaho. Mrs. Brown wasn't far behind. Christensen, the lawyer, recounted in a deposition what happened when the two women crossed paths.

"Mrs. Brown walked up towards her and grabbed her by the throat and threw her down, and intended to kill her. . . . [After] I separated them, they got up and commenced talking in a very low tone of voice . . . when Mrs. Brown grabbed her again. I separated them, and Mrs. Brown says, 'Let me alone, I'll kill her. . . .' Then Mrs. Bradley called out and says, 'Arthur, they are killing your Dolly—open the door. . . .' There was no response from the senator's room. Finally, Mrs.

Brown said, 'Arthur, open the door or I'll mash it in.' The door opened and when the two women went in . . . Arthur Brown called me, and said, 'Come in, I don't want to be left alone here with them.' "

During the night, Brown, whose wide mouth and high forehead made him look like a tropical fish, admitted fathering the son Mrs. Bradley had given birth to three years before, at which point, Christensen recalled, Mrs. Brown flew into a jealous rage. Thinking his wife might have murder in mind, Brown, in a decision that would have grave personal consequences, gave Mrs. Bradley a pistol for self-protection.

He also gave her his word he would get a divorce and that afterward the two would leave the United States and settle in Poland. But an escape to Europe turned out to be unnecessary. Mrs. Brown died of cancer in 1905. The next day, Brown phoned Mrs. Bradley, who was still married. "Now darling," he said, "go ahead . . . get your divorce and we will make this matter right."

While Mrs. Bradley did as she was told, Brown was in no hurry to make their relationship legal. A marriage date was set for June 1906, and Brown swore that "if I don't carry out my promise . . . I call upon God to avenge it." When the day arrived, however, he complained he was too ill to go through with the ceremony and it was called off.

Divorced, with four children—two of them supposedly fathered by Brown—Mrs. Bradley was desperate for Brown to marry her. "I simply broke down and begged him," she said later in court. "I told him I could never face the little children when they grew up. . . . I felt as if the future was very dark."

In one last attempt to get back on her feet, Mrs. Bradley informed her sister she planned to ask Brown for $2,000 so she could open a store in Nevada. At first, Brown seemed willing to pay the money, then abruptly changed his mind and left for Washington to argue a case before the Supreme Court.

Mrs. Bradley followed him, and on December 8, 1906, registered as "Mrs. A. Brown" at the old Raleigh Hotel where Brown was staying. In his room, she found several letters that made it clear he was planning to marry another woman. Mrs. Bradley was incensed, and when Brown returned, she was waiting for him.

The *Washington Star* reported that Mrs. Bradley "declared she could not remember any of the events following. She did not know Brown was shot until she seemed to be awakened as from a death by the sound of a [gun]. Brown had rushed toward her and grabbed her, Mrs. Bradley said, but she did not remember drawing the revolver, aiming it at Brown or pulling the trigger. She had never fired a revolver before in her life."

During questioning by the police, Mrs. Bradley said Brown had "not treated her properly." Before he died, Brown told a hospital nurse, "I never wronged that woman." But that's not how the public saw it.

The *Salt Lake Tribune,* predicting that Mrs. Bradley "will be acquitted of any charge which may be lodged against her in connection with the shooting," found no reason to sympathize with Brown.

Mrs. Bradley's trial for murder began in Washington on November 19, 1907, with lawyers announcing that her defense would be temporary insanity brought on by several abortions, one of which, they claimed, "was performed by Brown."

On the witness stand Mrs. Bradley wept repeatedly as she described her treatment by Brown, who denied in his will that he had ever intended to marry her and forbade the payment of any money to her or the children she said he had fathered.

"Did you shoot Senator Brown?" Mrs. Bradley's lawyer asked her.

"I do not know," she answered.

"Were you animated by any feeling of vengeance toward him at the time you went to his room?"

"Only of utter helplessness and dependence upon him," she said, "and of love in spite of the many disappointments."

The trial lasted twenty-one days, and when it was over the judge instructed the all-male jury to remember their duty under the law, reminding them that "All that is noble in us demands that the man should protect and rescue the woman, and when it appears that he has not only seduced but afterwards betrayed and abandoned her it is impossible for manly men to withhold their condemnation."

The jury's verdict: not guilty.

Ironically, the first person ever to use an insanity defense successfully was New York Rep. Daniel Sickles, who was put on trial in 1859 for shooting his wife's lover, the son of "Star-Spangled Banner" composer Francis Scott Key. That a politician could walk out of court a free man after killing someone only added to the general feeling that members of Congress could get away with murder.

Brown, on the other hand, was seen to have gotten just what he deserved. He was reviled in newspaper accounts of the trial. The *Star* reported that the jury's decision was greeted by courtroom spectators with cheers and applause. The *Salt Lake Tribune* said the not-guilty verdict "demonstrates the truth of the comments . . . made upon Brown's character."

Arthur Brown may have paid the ultimate price for his philandering, but how many other members of Congress have narrowly escaped a similar fate?

As for Mrs. Bradley, after the trial she returned to Salt Lake

City, where she lived quietly until the past came back to haunt her in 1915. While she was out of town on business, her oldest son, Matthew Bradley, was accidentally stabbed to death by his half-brother Arthur Brown Bradley, the illegitimate son Brown had cut out of his will. The two siblings had gotten into a fight over which one would do the dishes. Arthur Bradley was never charged.

Sen. Arthur Brown, a Utah Republican, is still the only member of Congress to be killed by a jealous mistress. *[The Utah State Historical Society]*

Lawyers for Mrs. Anne Bradley claimed she was temporarily insane when she shot Brown. *[Copyright The Washington Post; reprinted by permission of the D.C. Public Library]*

The Raleigh Hotel, once a love nest for lawmakers and their girlfriends, was Brown's last address. *[Historical Society of Washington, D.C.]*

2

White House
Couch Case

Many U.S. presidents have probably needed to have their heads examined, but only one—Woodrow Wilson—had his mind probed by Sigmund Freud.

Although the two never met, Freud believed Wilson was motivated by a classic Oedipus complex, a problem the twenty-eighth president himself readily admitted in a letter to his first wife. "I remember how I clung to mother 'til I was a great big fellow," he wrote, suggesting the new Mrs. Wilson might have a hard time replacing the old one.

Freud, who wrote a book on Wilson's psyche in 1932, thought it unlikely this son of a Calvinist minister had ever had sex with anyone before he married Ellen Axson in 1885. From then on, however, Wilson's special need for mothering females played a major role in both his public and private life.

For years, the main object of his extramarital attention was Mrs. Mary Peck, the estranged wife of a Massachusetts industrialist. Wilson was attracted to Mrs. Peck from the first time he met her in Bermuda during a three-week vacation in 1907, six years before he entered the White House.

Some politicians want women for sex. But Freud theorized that Wilson, whom he claimed actually feared other men, viewed all women, even his own three daughters, as "substitutes" for his doting and protective mother.

In this respect, Mrs. Peck proved to be the perfect companion, and Wilson poured his heart out to her. "There is an air about you," he wrote, "a directness, a simplicity, a free movement that links you with wild things that are . . . meant to be taken into one's confidence and loved."

By the time Mr. and Mrs. Peck finally got around to filing for a divorce, Wilson was running for president. There was talk that he might be named in the suit, with his many letters offered as evidence that he and Mrs. Peck had been lovers, but the Pecks' marriage ended quietly, and Wilson escaped the embarrassment of a messy scandal, even though he and Mrs. Peck may have only been friends.

"You can't cast a man as a Romeo who looks . . . like an apothecary's clerk," said Theodore Roosevelt, who ran for the White House in 1912 as a third-party candidate.

Wilson won the election, but when his wife, Ellen, died of kidney disease shortly afterward, he was so distraught that he told an acquaintance he wished someone would assassinate him. The president often spent days mourning alone in his room. His closest aides feared he might be losing his mind, but this made perfect sense to the father of psychiatry. Freud believed that Wilson, besides having a mother fixation, also had a Christ complex, leading him to conclude that the suffering president was right in his element.

Six months after his wife's death, Wilson was introduced to a forty-three-year-old Washington widow, Mrs. Edith Bolling Galt. Described as "a healthy, full-bosomed . . . woman of the upper middle-class," Mrs. Galt brought Wilson out of his depression, and before long he was madly in love with her. "Again he refound 'a center of quiet' for his life," wrote Freud, "and a mother's breast on which to rest."

As the public became aware of Wilson's new romance, opinion soon turned from sympathy to anger, and even suspicion of foul play. Had the president, best known for his mild-mannered moralizing, murdered his first wife in order to marry Mrs. Galt? Many considered it a distinct possibility. The announcement that the two planned to be married produced an immediate outbreak of humor on the subject, some of it so cruel it reportedly made Wilson cry. *What did Mrs. Galt do when the president proposed to her?* went one joke. *She fell out of bed.*

The public knew nothing of Wilson's psychological insecurities, or of how Mrs. Galt had transformed him from a grieving widower to a love-struck schoolboy. His decision to run for reelection in 1916 gave Republicans a chance to use the worst rumors about his sex life in the campaign. But when Wilson and Mrs. Galt suddenly married before the election, public opinion made another dramatic reversal. Americans adored the new first couple. Wilson easily won reelection, and with U.S. entry into World War I, the gossip about his private life ended.

The president took full advantage of events during and after the war to act out the role of savior, first declaring the purpose of the conflict was "to make the world safe for democracy," then virtually martyring himself to the cause of peace.

In late September 1919, exhaustion forced Wilson to shorten a trip to the West Coast, where he had been drumming up support for the League of Nations. A few weeks after returning to the White House, while shaving one morning, he suffered a massive stroke that permanently paralyzed his left side and severely affected his mental abilities.

Mrs. Wilson and White House physician Admiral Cary T.

Grayson decided that the American public should not be informed of the full extent of the president's illness, and the two devised an elaborate medical cover-up. The initial White House bulletin on Wilson's health, issued two hours after his stroke, said, "The president had a fairly good night," then added with no further comment that "his condition is not at all good this morning."

While Wilson saw no one for months, his wife functioned not only as his primary press agent but also as the de facto head of state, the same role Nancy Reagan and Hillary Clinton would be accused of playing many years later. The difference is that Edith really did run things. All outside communication to the president was submitted in letter form to Mrs. Wilson, who occasionally returned notes in her own handwriting saying what her husband had decided. She admitted in her memoirs that for the rest of his administration Wilson never read anything that she didn't approve of first.

For the public, kept purposely in the dark by the First Lady's deceit, Wilson's disappearance gave rise to wild speculation. With the chief executive nowhere in sight, rumors spread quickly that he had been kidnapped by Bolsheviks and poisoned by League of Nations opponents. One story was that he had gone mad. Bars on the upper-floor windows of the White House, originally installed to keep Teddy Roosevelt's children from falling out, were taken as proof that the president was a raving lunatic.

The man who should have been most interested in Wilson's state of health was Vice President Thomas Marshall, famous for once saying, "What this country needs is a good five-cent cigar." Marshall was terrified at the prospect of taking over the presidency, but with the cabinet believing reports that the president was getting better, his succession was never considered a serious possibility. In the meantime, Mrs. Wilson continued to run the government from the White

House, signing bills into law by holding the president's hand as she wrote his name.

In the months after his League of Nations proposal went down to defeat in the Senate, Wilson gradually recovered some of his physical abilities, but never all of his senses. Often, on automobile rides through Washington, the frail and aging president would instruct his Secret Service agents to pull over speeders so he could lecture them for disobeying the law, somehow a fitting occupation for a man who had always wanted to be the world's moral policeman.

Woodrow Wilson, with first wife, Ellen (second from left), and their three daughters, was dominated by women throughout his life. *[Library of Congress]*

Wilson and Edith Bolling Galt, his second wife, attend a baseball game. Before they were married, rumors of a sexual affair between the two made the president cry. *[Library of Congress]*

When a massive stroke in 1919 left Wilson permanently disabled, Edith took over the White House. She even signed legislation by holding the president's hand as she wrote his name. *[Library of Congress]*

DRIP DRY

The most famous piece of legislation Woodrow Wilson ever signed—or had signed for him after his stroke—was the Volstead Act, which made it illegal to manufacture, sell, or consume alcoholic beverages anywhere in the United States. But by the time Prohibition became the law of the land in 1919, Washington had already been officially dry for more than two years, thanks to another law, the Sheppard Act, named after abstemious Texas senator Morris Sheppard.

Washington's head start on the rest of the country was a boon for D.C. bootleggers. Local speakeasies were crowded with customers when the fad was just beginning in New York and Chicago.

Lawmakers on Capitol Hill, however, had their own private hideaways, where members of Congress gathered to imbibe. One drinking club was called the Bar Flies Association, a floating cocktail hour that met in a different House

Federal agents raid a Capitol Hill speakeasy. Prohibition did little to stop the flow of booze in Congress. *[Library of Congress]*

or Senate office every day. Another in-House bar known as the Board of Education was founded by Democrat John Nance Garner of Texas, who later became vice president under Franklin Roosevelt. "Boys, let's strike a blow for liberty," was Garner's favorite toast.

Besides being wholesale consumers of alcohol, politicians were also active in production and distribution. Two supposed teetotaling Republicans, congressmen Alfred Michaelson and Edward Everett Denison from Illinois, were caught with huge stashes of illegal liquor. Both convinced juries it belonged to someone else and got off. Not so lucky was Rep. John W. Langley, a Kentucky Republican who was convicted of running a booze business and sentenced to two years in prison.

Woodrow Wilson's successor, Warren G. Harding, was notorious for serving contraband cocktails to his friends during White House card games. But Herbert Hoover, a straight-laced Quaker determined to end drinking entirely, authorized the Justice Department to use paid informers to help curb the problem in Washington and elsewhere.

Herbert Hoover was so determined to put an end to bootlegging in Washington that he authorized paid informants to catch offenders. *[Library of Congress]*

On the Hill, a bootleg liquor business run by George L. Cassidy, otherwise known as "the man in the green hat," thrived for years, until Cassidy was arrested and his "little black book" confiscated by federal agents in 1930. Many members of Congress, claiming the executive branch was spying on them, vowed to keep on drinking no matter what the law said.

Their defiance continued until 1933, when Prohibition was finally repealed, although a special bill had to be passed to cancel the Sheppard Act so drinking could once again be legal in Washington.

3

The President's Pants
Are Missing

Warren G. Harding is often ranked with Richard Nixon as one of the century's worst presidents. But Harding had much more in common with John F. Kennedy, one of the most popular. Both men failed to complete their first term in the White House. Both died under suspicious circumstances. And both had insatiable appetites for sex that some conspiracy theorists believe played a major role in their deaths.

The first president elected after women received the right to vote, Harding's silent-movie-star good looks made him a virtual matinee idol when he took office in 1921. He was also the first chief executive to invite real movie stars to his inauguration, among them Al Jolson, a native Washingtonian. Like Kennedy, Harding was managed by people who understood the importance of political production values, which was fortunate, since Harding himself seemed completely incapable of uttering a sensible thought.

"I would like government to do all it can to mitigate; then, in understanding, in mutuality of interest, in concern for the common good, our tasks will be solved," he declared in his inaugural address.

Harding had been a newspaper editor in Marion, Ohio, when he married Florence Kling DeWolf, a divorcée five years older than he was and the daughter of the richest man in town. His new wife, known as the Duchess, took charge of Harding's business affairs. Starting by reorganizing the newsboys, one of whom was Norman Thomas, the future Socialist candidate for the presidency, she soon had the paper turning a handsome profit, which freed her husband to gladhand his way around the state.

In 1898, Harding was elected to the Ohio Senate. It was there he met dealmaker Harry Daugherty, who observed that the dashing Republican "looked like a president," an attribute that would eventually help Daugherty put Harding in the White House.

Meanwhile, Florence Harding had consulted an astrologer about her husband and was told he was "kind, intuitive and trustful of friends." She also learned that Harding would have "many clandestine love affairs," information that confirmed what she already suspected.

During most of the time he spent in Washington, first in the Senate and then in the White House, Harding carried on two affairs simultaneously: one with Carrie Phillips, the wife of a Marion businessman; the other with Nan Britton, who first developed a crush on Harding in his late forties, when she was fourteen and Harding's sister was her high school English teacher.

The relationship with Mrs. Phillips lasted for fifteen years, until Harding's campaign for the presidency in 1920 made it impossible for him to keep seeing her. On one occasion, after learning what her husband was up to, the Duchess tried to chase Mrs. Phillips away from a political rally by throwing a piano stool at her. Leaders of the Republican Party had a better idea. They paid Mrs. Phillips $20,000 for Harding's old love letters and sent her on an extended world tour with a hefty monthly stipend.

Harding's relationship with Nan Britton was consummated shortly after he was elected to the U.S. Senate in 1915. Britton had moved from Ohio to New York to attend secretarial school, and described her first romantic encounter with the man of her dreams in her tell-all memoirs, *The President's Daughter,* published in 1927:

"The bridal chamber of the Manhattan Hotel was, to me, a very lovely room, and in view of the fact that we had scarcely closed the door behind us when we shared our first kiss, it seemed sweetly appropriate. The bed, which we did not disturb, stood upon a dais and the furnishings were in keeping with the general refinement of [the] atmosphere. I shall never forget how Mr. Harding kept saying, after each kiss, 'God! . . . God, Nan!' in high diminuendo, nor how he pleaded in a tense voice, 'Oh, Dearie, tell me it isn't hateful to you to have me kiss you.' And as I kissed him . . . I thought that he surpassed even my gladdest dreams of him."

Before long, Harding was panting for more and sending Britton love letters that gave full expression to his passion:

My darling, Nan,
  I love you more than the world, and I want you to belong to me. Could you belong to me, dearie? I want you . . . I need you so.

After the United States entered World War I, Harding's obsessive interest in sex carried over into foreign relations. Like most red-blooded Americans he hated the Germans, and one of the things he detested most, he confided to Britton, was their scientific approach to procreation.

"Mr. Harding vouchsafed the information he had recently

acquired in Washington that the Germans were actually attempting to create children by injecting male serum, taken at the proper temperature, into the female without the usual medium of sexual contact. He denounced this method of propagation as 'German madness' and affirmed that in his belief children should come only through mutual love-desire."

Given his strong feelings on the subject and the fact that he and Britton were having sex anywhere they could find the space, including his cramped Senate office, Harding's young mistress soon became pregnant. He supported their child, a daughter he never saw, with payments of $500 a month.

In days when sex was a touchy subject in the press, Harding's dalliances never became a presidential campaign issue, but the charge by some that he had "Negro blood" did. Rumors had circulated around Marion for years that Harding had black ancestors. So convinced was his wife's father of the rumors that he threatened to blow Harding's head off if he married his daughter. Despite an effort by southern Democrats to rekindle race fears in the 1920 election, Harding won by a landslide, though his campaign slogan, "A Return to Normalcy," hardly described the new president's love life.

The Duchess was aware of her husband's philandering, yet the Nan Britton affair, thanks to Harding's expert planning, remained a secret, proving the otherwise bumbling commander in chief was at least adept at one thing. Of far greater concern to his wife than his womanizing was Harding's heart condition, which could not have been helped by his rigorous schedule of sexual activity. One Washington doctor who met the president at a dinner party in 1922, noting all the classic symptoms of advanced heart disease, gave him six more months to live.

Some historians suspect that Mrs. Harding enlisted White House physician, Dr. Charles Sawyer, in her ongoing surveillance of her husband. But Harding, an expert at deception, may have outsmarted them both.

"Gee, Nan," he complained, "they bother me to death . . . looking at my tongue and feeling my pulse. Why a fellow can't be alone a minute. Now what I really need is some of your treatment." And with the aid of the White House Secret Service, who helped Britton sneak past the Duchess and the Doc, that's what he got.

The couple's favorite place to have sex in the Executive Mansion was a closet reached from the Oval Office by what they called the "secret passage." In early 1923, the president and Britton met there for the last time.

"We lingered long inside the closed door . . . before we left the executive office," Britton remembered. "Little would I have actually believed, despite the chills of premonition that I had experienced during that visit, that never again would we stand like this together upon this earth."

With the presidential election a year away, Harding's handlers thought he could use a coast-to-coast political trip. The trip, which included a steamship cruise to Alaska, started in Washington's Union Station on June 20, 1923. Accompanying the president were White House staff, Secret Service men, and a train car full of reporters. The Duchess and Dr. Sawyer came along too.

On the return leg of the journey, after Harding nearly collapsed while he was making a speech in Seattle, he was rushed to San Francisco's Palace Hotel and put into bed. Sawyer blamed the problem on food poisoning, but other physicians attending the president thought he'd had a heart attack.

One evening, while his wife was alone with him in his room, Harding broke out in a cold sweat, slumped over, and died. Sawyer claimed the president had succumbed to a stroke, and since Mrs. Harding would not permit the president's body to be autopsied, that was given as the official cause of death.

But Sawyer's opinion caused an immediate controversy. Had Harding died from a heart attack, as some medical specialists believed? Or had he been poisoned by his jealous wife, possibly with Sawyer's help, as many people suspected?

The theory gained credibility when a little over a year later Sawyer died just as Harding had. The only person with him at the time was Florence Harding, the late president's widow.

Warren Harding demonstrates one of his many leading-man poses designed to drive women wild. *[Library of Congress]*

Harding attends a horse show with his wife, Florence (right), and two attractive Washington socialites. *[Library of Congress]*

Harding's body is loaded on a train in San Francisco for the trip back east. Did Florence commit murder? *[Library of Congress]*

THE TEAPOT DOME CAPER

A total of three cabinet members have invoked the Fifth Amendment to avoid incriminating themselves during congressional hearings. One was Samuel Pierce, Ronald Reagan's secretary of Housing and Urban Development, who was under investigation for corruption.

The other two were both members of Warren Harding's administration: Secretary of the Navy Edwin Denby and Interior Secretary Albert Fall, who went on to achieve another distinction. Fall, the recipient of kickbacks in exchange for no-bid drilling leases at government oil reserves in Elk Hills, California, and Teapot Dome, Wyoming, was the first cabinet secretary to go to jail.

4

Experience Counts

In his first campaign for mayor of Boston in 1913, Democratic representative James Michael Curley ran against the incumbent, Mayor John F. Fitzgerald, the grandfather of future president John F. Kennedy. Curley knew that Fitzgerald was friendly with a roadhouse cigarette girl named Elizabeth "Toodles" Ryan, and as election day approached, he went into action.

First, a letter arrived at Mayor Fitzgerald's house advising him to drop out of the race or the Toodles affair would be made public. When Fitzgerald, known as "Honey Fitz" for his tenor voice, spent too much time mulling over the long-term effects of his decision, Curley announced plans to give a series of public lectures, one to be called "Libertines in History: From Henry the Eighth to the Present" and another entitled "Great Lovers in History: From Cleopatra to Toodles." Fitzgerald got the message and announced his retirement.

Curley won, and during the next forty years he would become one of the most corrupt politicians in American history.

Over his long career, Curley went to jail twice. The first time was in 1904, when he and a friend were found guilty of taking civil service exams for two Irish immigrants. As mayor of Boston and later as governor of Massachusetts, he would do a lot worse. Curley was accused, though never convicted, of bribery, fraud, and corruption. It wasn't until he returned to Congress in 1943 that the law finally caught up with him.

During his first four years in the mayor's office he built himself a magnificent twenty-one-room mansion, complete with carved mahogany doors, Italian marble fireplaces, and a two-story bronze chandelier from the Austro-Hungarian Embassy in Washington. That he did it all on an annual salary of $10,000 is a testament to his political philosophy never to take a quarter from anybody who couldn't afford it.

Curley, in fact, made a fortune in kickbacks from city contracts. He knew that all politics is local and never lost touch with the poor Irish voters who kept reelecting him, many no doubt just to listen to his speeches. According to biographer Jack Beatty, most of those were plagiarized from the *Congressional Record* by his "speechwriter," Standish Willcox, who would add quotes from Shakespeare, Milton, and others to give Curley's discourse the class his poor Irish constituents envied in Yankee Republicans, otherwise known as "our Brahmin overlords."

"There is no fear of an exposé," reasoned Willcox. "While many people get the *Congressional Record,* few ... ever read it."

Like Huey "Kingfish" Long of Louisiana, another famous politician of the day, Curley knew how to dress the part. With a taste for white suits and fur coats, he was a master of the hyperbolic fashion statement. He may have called himself

"Mayor of the Poor," but that never stopped him from wearing spats.

Turning his back on the Irish Catholic candidate, Al Smith, Curley supported Franklin Roosevelt for president in 1932. He hoped to get a cabinet post or the ambassadorship to Italy, ruled by Benito Mussolini, one of his political heroes. But after the election, when Roosevelt offered to make him ambassador to Poland instead, Curley blew up. "If Poland is such a goddamn interesting place, why don't you resign the presidency and take it yourself," he told FDR, turning down the post.

During his first two terms in Congress (1911–14), Curley had remained a member of the Boston City Council, a move that he claimed saved the city the expense of calling a special election to fill his seat. In reality, it allowed him to keep his hand in local affairs, where it could easily be filled with payoffs and bribes.

By the time he was voted back to Congress in 1943, the big money had moved to Washington. The government was spending billions on the war effort, and Curley, in his never-ending quest for a quick buck, lent his name to a shady firm set up ostensibly to help small businesses get federal contracts. The company was little more than a front to swindle contractors, and for his role in the scheme, in 1947, Curley was found guilty of fraud and sentenced to eighteen months in prison.

While his trial went on, Curley busied himself by campaigning for his fourth term as mayor of Boston. He sought the job at the age of seventy on the advice of Joseph P. Kennedy, anxious to free a local congressional seat for his son John. In return for Curley's promise to resign from the House if he was reelected to run the city, the elder Kennedy agreed to pick up the tab for his mayoral race.

As expected, Curley easily won the election. Boston voters, 60 percent of whom cast their ballots for him, seemed unfazed by charges of corruption and wartime profiteering. Calling him "the amazing Mr. Curley," the *Boston Post* reluctantly conceded that "he is the personal hero of a substantial and loyal segment of the city's population."

Bostonians who voted for him year in and year out knew Curley was a crook. But he was *their* crook. In that capacity he could be even more devious than Joe Kennedy. Following the election, Curley reneged on his agreement, and since there was no law against it, he threatened to keep his congressional job.

A prison sentence soon put an end to those plans. With Curley languishing behind bars, all but one member of the Massachusetts delegation in Congress signed a petition asking President Harry Truman to issue an executive pardon. Conspicuous by its absence was the name of Rep. John F. Kennedy, whose family was just as happy to keep their old nemesis safely locked up.

The Last Hurrah, a novel by Edwin O'Connor, turned Curley into a sympathetic figure, a reputation sustained by his final campaign for mayor of Boston in 1951, which ended in crushing defeat. But even though everyone knew he would lose, people turned out just to hear him speak.

"If they love me so much," he griped about one cheering crowd, "why won't the sons of bitches vote for me?"

James Michael Curley served four terms in Congress and two terms in jail. He lost his bid for a fifth term as mayor of Boston in 1951. *[The Rare Book Collection, Holy Cross Library]*

Curley and his wife, Gertrude, demonstrate the lavish lifestyle that politics made possible. *[The Rare Book Collection, Holy Cross Library]*

MEMBERS OF CONGRESS BEHIND BARS
1900–1995

Year Charged	Member	Crime and Punishment

1904 Sen. Joseph R. Burton (R-Kans), bribery. Convicted. Sentenced to five months in prison.

1924 Rep. John W. Langley (R-Ky), violating National Prohibition Act. Convicted. Sentenced to two years in prison.

1931 Rep. Harry E. Rowbottom (R-Ind), accepting bribes. Convicted. Sentenced to one year and one day in prison.

1934 Rep. George E. Foulkes (D-Mich), conspiracy to assess political contributions from postmasters. Convicted. Sentenced to eighteen months in prison.

1936 Rep. John Hoeppel (D-Calif), influence peddling. Convicted. Sentenced to four months in prison.

1946 Rep. James Curley (D-Mass), mail fraud, conspiracy. Convicted. Sentenced to eighteen months in prison.

1947 Rep. Andrew J. May (R-Ky), conspiracy to defraud the U.S. government and accepting bribes. Convicted. Sentenced to eighteen months in prison.

1948 Rep. J. Parnell Thomas (R-NJ), conspiring to defraud the U.S. government, payroll padding, receiving salary kickbacks. Convicted. Sentenced to eighteen months in prison.

1956 Rep. Thomas J. Lane (D-Mass), federal income tax evasion. Pleaded guilty. Sentenced to four months in prison and fined $10,000.

1969 Rep. Hugh J. Addonizio (D-NJ), extortion, conspiracy, income tax evasion. Convicted. Sentenced to ten years in prison.

Experience Counts

Year Charged	Member	Crime and Punishment
1970	Rep. John V. Dowdy (D-Tex), conspiracy, conflict of interest, perjury, bribery. Convicted. Sentenced to eighteen months in prison.	
1972	Rep. Cornelius Gallagher (D-NJ), income tax evasion, perjury, conspiracy. Pleaded guilty to tax evasion. Sentenced to sixteen months in prison.	
1973	Rep. Bertram L. Podell (D-NY), conspiracy, bribery, perjury. Pleaded guilty. Sentenced to six months in prison.	
1973	Rep. Frank J. Brasco (D-NY), conspiracy to receive bribes. Convicted. Sentenced to three months in prison.	
1975	Rep. Andrew Hinshaw (R-Calif), soliciting a bribe, bribery, embezzlement, conspiracy, misuse of public funds and petty theft. Convicted. Sentenced to one year in prison.	
1976	Rep. James F. Hastings (R-NY), kickbacks, mail fraud. Convicted. Served fourteen months in jail.	
1977	Rep. Richard A. Tonry (D-La), receiving illegal campaign contributions, obstructing justice. Pleaded guilty. Served six months in jail.	
1977	Rep. Richard T. Hanna (D-Calif), conspiracy to defraud the U.S. government. Pleaded guilty. Served eighteen months in jail.	
1978	Rep. Charles C. Diggs (D-Mich), mail fraud and perjury. Convicted. Sentenced to three years in prison.	
1979	Rep. Michael "Ozzie" Myers (D-Pa), bribery and conspiracy (ABSCAM). Convicted. Sentenced to three years in jail.	
1980	Sen. Harrison Williams (D-NJ), bribery and conspiracy (ABSCAM). Convicted. Sentenced to three years.	
1980	Rep. Raymond F. Lederer (D-Pa), conspiracy, influence peddling, bribery (ABSCAM). Convicted. Jailed for one year.	

Year Charged	Member	Crime and Punishment

1980   Rep. John Jenrette (D-SC), bribery, conspiracy (AB-SCAM). Convicted. Served two years in prison.

1980   Rep. Frank Thompson (D-NJ), influence peddling, bribery (ABSCAM). Convicted. Sentenced to thirteen months in prison.

1980   Rep. John Murphy (D-NY), influence peddling, bribery (ABSCAM). Convicted. Sentenced to three years in prison.

1980   Rep. Richard Kelly (R-Fla), bribery and conspiracy (ABSCAM). Convicted. Sentenced to thirteen months in prison.

1983   Rep. George Hansen (R-Idaho), filing false financial disclosure statements. Convicted. Sentenced to fifteen months in prison.

1988   Rep. Mario Biaggi (D-NY), obstructing justice, tax evasion, conspiracy, extortion, accepting bribes (Wedtech). Convicted. Sentenced to twenty-six months in prison.

1988   Rep. Pat Swindall (R-Ga), perjury. Convicted. Sentenced to one year in jail.

1989   Rep. Donald E. "Buz" Lukens (R-Ohio), contributing to the delinquency of a minor. Convicted. Jailed for nine days.

1991   Rep. Nick Mavroules (D-Mass), bribery, tax evasion, and influence peddling. Pleaded guilty. Sentenced to fifteen months in jail.

1993   Rep. Albert Bustamante (D-Tex), racketeering and accepting an illegal gratuity. Convicted. Sentenced to three years in prison.

1993   Rep. Larry Smith (D-Fla), income tax and campaign reporting violations. Convicted. Sentenced to three months in jail.

1994   Rep. Carrol Hubbard (D-Ky), misappropriation of funds. Convicted. Sentenced to three years in prison.

Experience Counts

Year Charged	Member	Crime and Punishment
1994	Rep. Carl Perkins (D-Ky), filing false financial disclosure statement. Pleaded guilty. Sentenced to twenty-one months in prison.	
1995	Rep. Mel Reynolds (D-Ill), having sex with a minor, soliciting child pornography, obstructing justice. Convicted. Sentenced to five years in prison.	

Rep. John Jenrette, bribery.
[U.S. House of Representatives]

Rep. Pat Swindall, perjury.
[Roll Call]

Rep. Charles Diggs, mail fraud.
[U.S. House of Representatives]

Rep. Nick Mavroules, influence
peddling. *[Roll Call]*

Rep. Donald "Buz" Lukens, sex with a female minor. *[Roll Call]*

Rep. Carrol Hubbard, misappropriation of funds. *[Roll Call]*

5

The First Family's Roommates

Presidential historians are still trying to figure out who slept with whom during the twelve years Franklin D. Roosevelt occupied the White House.

Two people for certain never shared the same bed. Franklin and Eleanor ceased having sex together sometime between 1916 and 1918, after the birth of their sixth child when Eleanor discovered that her husband and her social secretary, Lucy Mercer, were having an affair. Bowing to pressure from his domineering mother, who threatened to disinherit her son if he got divorced, FDR promised never to see Lucy again, but that did little to repair his marriage. It was also a pledge that he often broke, and for years he and Lucy met secretly, even in the White House when Eleanor was away from Washington.

Despite the onset of crippling polio in 1921, FDR remained sexually operative. After Lucy's marriage to Winthrop Rutherford, a wealthy New York aristocrat, she and Roosevelt continued seeing one another behind their spouses' backs. As was the case with Warren Harding and his frequent philandering, the Secret Service and White House staff looked the other way during the president's meetings with Lucy. FDR's daughter Anna, always loyal to her father, also helped to cover up his amorous comings and goings.

Roosevelt's visits with Lucy became more frequent during the war years, when tight presidential security made concealing their whereabouts a matter of executive protection. A favorite spot to rendezvous was Warm Springs, Georgia, where FDR went for rest and rehabilitation. Conveniently, Lucy's husband owned an estate in nearby Aiken, South Carolina. Lucy and Roosevelt were together in Warm Springs when the president died on April 12, 1945, though it would be many years before that information was ever made public.

Lucy Mercer may have been Roosevelt's true love, but his day-to-day mistress was his White House secretary, the appropriately named Missy LeHand. Missy not only took dictation, she lived with the president as his "wife," and everyone from servants to cabinet officials treated her as substitute First Lady. Eleanor, who had loathed Lucy, seemed to accept Missy, who ran the White House as if she lived there, which she did, in a small suite not far from the president's bedroom. Eleanor slept in another part of the family quarters.

To emphasize her place in his life, Roosevelt provided in his will that half of his nearly $2 million estate go to "my friend Marguerite A. LeHand."

Missy lived and worked in the White House until 1941, when she suffered a stroke that left her severely debilitated. Her intimate relationship with the president came to a sad end when she was moved from a Washington hospital to her sister's home in Massachusetts, where she suffered a second stroke and died in 1944, less than a year before Roosevelt's own death.

* * *

The First Family's Roommates

Eleanor's sex life was even more unconventional than her husband's. During FDR's presidency, the Roosevelts may have lived under the same roof, but they never lived as a couple. Eleanor, like her husband, also had a White House love interest.

Lorena Hickok was an Associated Press reporter when she and the future First Lady met during the 1932 presidential campaign. The two were instantly attracted to one another. Hickok, a heavyset woman with a pronounced masculine walk, was like many of Eleanor's close female friends, socially committed and sexually liberated.

In her memoirs, Hickok admitted that after meeting Eleanor, whom she was assigned to cover during the campaign, she soon lost her journalistic objectivity. In a matter of weeks the women became inseparable. For Roosevelt's first two terms, Eleanor and Hick, as she was known, carried on a long-distance relationship, traveling back and forth between Washington and New York to see one another and writing thousands of letters, many of them sentimental and others undeniably erotic.

Shortly before Roosevelt's first inauguration, Hick had given Eleanor a sapphire ring, which soon became her most prized possession: "Hick, darling," she wrote, "I want to put my arms around you. I ache to hold you close. Your ring is a great comfort. I look at it and think she does love me. . . ."

In another letter, Eleanor talks of longing to kiss Hick good night but having to content herself with kissing her picture instead.

Once, after Hick had called her at the White House, Eleanor wrote: "Oh, how good it was to hear your voice. . . . It was so inadequate to try to tell you what it meant. Jimmy [James Roosevelt, her son] was near and I couldn't say Je t'aime and je t'adore. . . . I go to sleep thinking of you. . . ."

Hick, anxious to see Eleanor, wrote back: "Funny how even the dearest face will fade away in time. Most clearly I remember your eyes, with a kind of teasing smile in them and the feeling of that soft spot just northwest of the corner of your mouth against my lips."

Some historians, like Doris Kearns Goodwin, have tried to explain the letters between Eleanor and Hick as typical "girl talk" for the 1930s and 1940s. But if the sentiments expressed were typical, why was Eleanor so concerned that her adult son not hear her tell Hick how much she loved her over the phone? And why would Roosevelt adviser Thomas Corcoran, who knew about the contents of the correspondence, have thought the letters should be burned to protect Eleanor's reputation?

Probably unaware that Eleanor and Hick were lovers, Roosevelt, who warned his wife to be wary of crafty female reporters like Hickok, soon lost his temper at the mere mention of her name. "I want that woman kept out of this house," he fumed, but Eleanor flatly refused to comply.

In a day when most people would have been aghast at their behavior, Eleanor and Hick not only enjoyed a long-term attachment but seemed to share a sense of bravado at violating what was then one of society's strictest taboos.

In 1941, Eleanor invited Hick to move into the White House. Her bedroom was located right across the hall from Eleanor's, giving them the opportunity to be together whenever they liked. For a while, the First Family was in reality *two* couples. The president had his live-in companion, Missy, and his wife had hers, Lorena Hickok.

As the First Lady's travels took her across the country, she often brought along Hick, whose newspaper skills were an obvious help when it came to preparing reports for the president. Hick, who had given up her career in journalism to be with Eleanor, also went on her own government assignments, updating officials in Washington on the progress of federal relief projects.

Hick is credited with bringing the naturally reserved Eleanor Roosevelt out of her shell. "You have taught me more than you know," Eleanor wrote to her. "You've made me so much more of a person just to be worthy of you."

But as the First Lady's sense of independence grew, her relationship with Hick changed. Hickok, having been jilted once when a woman she had lived with ran off with an old boyfriend, became increasingly possessive of Eleanor. "It would be so much better, wouldn't it, if I didn't love you so much," wrote Hick.

Eleanor had shown signs she was tiring of her friend's jealousy even before Hick came to live in the White House. Maybe a husband might have satisfied her constant "cravings," an exasperated Eleanor lashed out at her lover.

In any case, by the early 1940s, their passions had cooled. And though they stayed close for the rest of their lives, when Hick moved from Washington to New York in 1945, any romance between them was over.

Franklin and Eleanor Roosevelt stopped having sex with each other, but neither one gave up fooling around. *[Library of Congress]*

Missy LeHand, Roosevelt's secretary for more than twenty years, was FDR's real Washington "wife." *[UPI/Bettmann Newsphotos]*

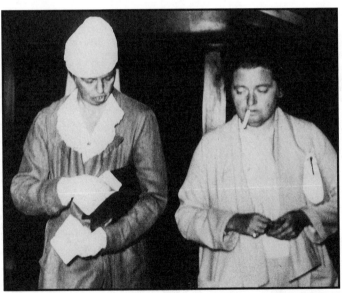

Eleanor and her love interest, Lorena Hickok (right), shared more than across-the-hall rooms at the White House. *[UPI/ Bettmann Newsphotos]*

WHO INVITED THIS GUY?

FDR's New Deal attracted to Washington some of the best minds in America. But it also brought with it a Democratic congressman from Seattle named Marion Zioncheck, one of the most deranged lawmakers ever to serve in the House.

The trouble began in December 1935, when the Polish-born Zioncheck, halfway through his second term, subleased an apartment belonging to Mrs. Pamela Schuyler Young, a widow who was leaving town on a lengthy trip to South America. No sooner had Zioncheck moved in than other tenants started complaining about loud music and all-night parties. During the next four months, the thirty-five-year-old congressman was arrested by D. C. police for speeding, drunk driving, and assaulting an officer. But the worst was yet to come.

Fearing that Mrs. Young's antique collection might not be in the best of care, the resident manager wired her in South America to return to Washington as fast as she could. When she arrived, she found that Zioncheck, who was on his honeymoon in Puerto Rico, had wrecked her apartment. Furniture and windows were broken, silverware was missing, and according to a police report, "more than 100 empty liquor bottles were seen on the premises."

Determined to save what was left of her belongings, Mrs. Young moved back into the apartment. She also began legal proceedings to evict Zioncheck and sue him for damages. That tactic did not sit well with the newlyweds, and when they got home, a battle royal ensued. After Mrs. Young refused to leave, Zioncheck's wife, Rubye, wrestled her to the floor; then her husband took over and dragged her into the hallway.

"Look, she's making a touchdown," Zioncheck told several reporters gathered at the scene.

49

A warrant was issued for Zioncheck, who was taken into custody the next day when police found him tossing his clothes out of the apartment window. As he was led from the building, the congressman, stripped to the waist and barefoot, yelled to a crowd of onlookers, "Oh, where is my crown of thorns?"

The story of Zioncheck's escapades made front-page headlines across the country. There were speaking invitations from New York and Chicago. Capitol Hill bars even began serving a drink, supposedly invented by its namesake, called the "Zioncheck zipper," equal parts rye whiskey and honey with a sprig of mint. In Pittsburgh, Mayor William McNair, who had recently announced plans to be a third-party candidate for president, named Zioncheck as his running mate.

After Rep. Marion Zioncheck ran away from a mental hospital, Capitol Hill cops escorted him out of Washington. *[Copyright Washington Post; reprinted by permission of the D.C. Public Library]*

Meanwhile, back in Washington, Zioncheck had posted bond and was on the loose. Driving his car down the wrong side of the street, he pulled up to the White House and dropped off a bag full of empty beer bottles as a gift to Franklin Roosevelt. He was arrested again, only this time he was sent to a hospital for mental observation.

Zioncheck's wife had him transferred to the Pratt Institute, a private sanitarium outside of Baltimore, but a few days later, he escaped and hitchhiked to Washington, where he hid out in his office. Claiming congressional immunity, Capitol police prevented the D.C. police from taking Zioncheck away, until the House sergeant-at-arms, Kenneth Romney, negotiated safe passage to Union Station and put him on a train for Washington State.

The final episode of the Marion Zioncheck saga took place in Seattle. Facing stiff opposition in the congressional primary, not to mention his long-shot campaign for the vice presidency, Zioncheck grew more and more despondent. On August 6, with a dozen opponents after his House seat, he told friends he was thinking about dropping out of the race. No one thought he meant it literally. But that evening, after writing a suicide note attacking America's "unfair economic system," he jumped out of the fifth-floor window of his campaign headquarters.

On Capitol Hill many speculated on what made Zioncheck go off the deep end.

"He left here with a serious persecution complex," said Romney after hearing the news of Zioncheck's death, adding that the erratic congressman never seemed to understand how Washington worked.

6

Prodigal Sons

The sons of Joseph P. Kennedy grew up believing the world was their sexual playground. And no wonder. Joe senior's longtime love affair with movie actress Gloria Swanson, often conducted in full view of his family, provided his male offspring with an at-home how-to course in marital infidelity. From the time they were old enough to imitate their philandering father, the four Kennedy boys—Joe junior, John, Bobby, and Ted—were picking up and discarding girlfriends with a devil-may-care abandon that made the old man proud.

Sex was like business for the elder Kennedy, who made his fortune in banking, and he took his work very seriously. In her autobiography, Swanson describes the first time Joe joined her in bed: "He moved so quickly that his mouth was on mine before either of us could speak," she wrote. "With one hand he held the back of my head, with the other he stroked my body and pulled my kimono. He kept insisting in a drawn-out moan, 'No longer, no longer, now.' He was like a roped horse . . . racing to be free. After a hasty climax he lay beside me, stroking my hair. Apart from his guilty, passionate mutterings, he [said] nothing cogent."

With his wife, Rose, keeping a dutiful distance, her husband conducted a parade of most-favored mistresses through the Kennedy compound. He set a high standard for his sons, and each did his best to measure up.

At the time of his death in a plane crash during World War II, Joe junior, handpicked by his father to be the first Irish Catholic president, was having a very public affair with a married woman. Young Joe's untimely death meant that John would be the number one son, and even before the war was over, his father had Jack's political future all figured out.

The work already done on Joe junior's behalf would serve to put his young brother in Congress. Yet, Jack was a reluctant candidate, not because he didn't want to serve in Washington but because holding public office seemed a lot less interesting than chasing women—that is, until he realized he could do both at the same time.

During an earlier trip to Washington, Jack had an affair with a twice-married newspaper reporter, Inga Arvad. The twenty-eight-year-old Danish woman was said to be the one true love of his life. But the relationship ended badly, thanks in large part to intervention by Joe senior, who thought Arvad, once suspected of spying, was not marriage material for a Kennedy.

After the war, JFK's romantic interests, like his father's, tended toward Hollywood. The object of his interest was actress Gene Tierney, then married to fashion designer Oleg Cassini. Kennedy may not have destroyed Cassini's marriage all by himself, though he certainly didn't help save it. That thought must have occurred to Joe senior when the playboy designer started hanging around Jacqueline Kennedy shortly after JFK won the presidential election in 1960.

Suspecting Cassini might have revenge in mind, and remembering his own affair with Gloria Swanson right under her husband's nose, the Kennedy patriarch tried to ward off the Italian, thereby saving his son the embarrassment he had caused Cassini fifteen years earlier.

Cassini, however, wasn't interested in sex. He wanted the White House fashion account. Once convinced the designer was on the level, Joe happily agreed to pay the bills while Jackie and Oleg went about the task of creating the look the world would forever associate with Camelot.

Around the same time, rumors began circulating in Washington that John Kennedy had secretly married and divorced a New York socialite six years before he wed Jacqueline Bouvier in 1953. As the story gathered steam, the Kennedy family went into a prevent defense. *Newsweek* reporter and JFK friend Ben Bradlee wrote an article citing FBI evidence that the rumors were politically motivated, and they gradually died out. Some reporters smelled a cover-up, particularly since the president approved the *Newsweek* article before it was published. Bradlee, who went on to become executive editor of the *Washington Post,* later said that everything may have been based on a big misunderstanding. "Probably Joe Kennedy [JFK's older brother] used to screw this girl, and that's how the connection was made," he explained. While Bradlee was helping to bury rumors of one John Kennedy sexcapade, several others were in progress, one of them with Bradlee's own sister-in-law, Mary Pinchot Meyer, who reportedly introduced the president to LSD.

Kennedy's insatiable need for female companionship might, today, be called an addiction. To those around him at the time, the women were simply part and parcel of the presidency. So much so that the Secret Service even managed the traffic flow.

Kennedy's most dangerous affair was with Judy Campbell, who also happened to be the girlfriend of Chicago mafia boss

Sam Giancana. The love triangle was discovered and subsequently broken up by FBI director J. Edgar Hoover, whose own sex life would later come under scrutiny. Recent revelations suggest that Hoover was a homosexual, given to attending orgies, dressing up in women's clothing, and calling himself "Mary." Hoover had several love affairs of his own that raised questions as serious as Kennedy's did. One was with Clyde Tolson, his top assistant at the FBI. Another involved attorney Roy Cohn, a former aide to Sen. Joseph McCarthy, the famous communist hunter in the 1950s.

Although Hoover saw the danger posed by Kennedy's affair with Campbell, dropping her from the presidential rotation hardly made a difference, since there were many others to take her place.

Marilyn Monroe and JFK had an affair that got so personal Monroe was thinking at one point she might replace Jackie as First Lady. One of the things Jack and Marilyn apparently enjoyed was making love in the bathtub at Peter Lawford's Santa Monica beach house. Lawford, then Kennedy's brother-in-law, is said to have shot pictures of the two at JFK's request as mementos of the occasion.

As Monroe got more and more demanding of John Kennedy's time and attention, Bobby stepped in to help separate them and, some believe, fell madly in love with the sex goddess himself. Monroe, whose daily diet of drugs read like a hospital inventory, was constantly threatening to kill herself, and affairs with the two Kennedy brothers may have been all that was needed to push her over the edge. At the time of her suicide there were rumors that Monroe was going to tell all about her relationship with the president. If so, whatever she had to say is sealed in a vault at Westwood Cemetery in Los Angeles, Marilyn's final resting place.

Ted Kennedy, the baby of the family, has made up for his low-man-on-the-totem-pole status by not only outliving all of his brothers but outdoing them in scandalous exposés. Starting in 1969, when he left the scene of a car wreck in which companion Mary Jo Kopechne was drowned, Ted Kennedy's life story could be written in tabloid headlines. There have been drunken bar fights, sexual assaults, and allegations, never proven, of a serious cocaine habit, now reportedly cured.

Once, when a picture of Ted appeared in the *National Enquirer,* showing him on top of a woman in a boat, Sen. Howell Heflin of Alabama remarked, "Well, I see Kennedy has changed his position on offshore drilling."

In 1987, Ted caused more talk when he threw a Christmas party for his Capitol Hill staff and showed up in drag dressed as Fawn Hall, the White House secretary of Iran-contra fame.

Ted Kennedy, in the words of one Washington reporter, was "off the reservation," an observation Ted himself confirmed one night in 1985, when he and fellow party animal, Sen. Chris Dodd of Connecticut, once called the only person in the Senate who was a bad influence on Kennedy, assaulted a waitress at La Brasserie, a restaurant on Capitol Hill.

Kennedy and Dodd, according to eyewitness accounts, were finishing dinner and drinks in a private room. Their dates, two young blondes, left the table to visit the bathroom. A waitress arrived, and Kennedy threw her on Dodd's lap. He then got on top and began rubbing his genital area against the woman. When her screams attracted other restaurant workers, Kennedy jumped up, and the frightened waitress got away. The evening ended with Kennedy and Dodd, surrounded by broken dishes, arguing over which one would pay the bill.

In 1991, it was Ted Kennedy who was with his nephew Willie Smith when Smith was accused of raping a woman the two had met in a Palm Beach bar.

Wisely, Ted remarried before his reelection campaign in 1994, a race many political observers felt he might lose without some effort to reform his life. Three years before, during a speech in Boston, Ted apologized to Massachusetts voters for his past mistakes and acknowledged the time had come to change his behavior.

"I recognize my shortcomings—the faults in the conduct of my private life," he said. "I realize that I alone am responsible for them, and I am the one who must confront them."

John Kennedy was the most promiscuous president in American history, which was fortunate for his brother Robert (left), who often got the leftovers, including prize reject Marilyn Monroe. *[U.S. Information Agency]*

Ted Kennedy and Senate colleague Christopher Dodd once held the distinction of being Washington's most out-of-control party animals. *[Roll Call]*

The wild life apparently behind him, Ted has settled down with his second wife, Victoria Reggie, and concentrated on gaining weight. *[Roll Call]*

7

All the Way
with LBJ

Just as the Kennedy sons were aimed into politics by their ambitious father, Lyndon Johnson's mother and her thwarted ambitions played a key role in shaping her son's desire for political success. Growing up poor, but instilled with an obsessive desire to get ahead, Johnson became an expert seducer, in both the political and the romantic sense.

He first came to Washington in 1932 to work as a congressional staffer. Before long, though, he was planning a political career of his own. Step one was to marry Lady Bird Taylor, the daughter of a wealthy Austin family. The money Lady Bird provided helped to fund Johnson's election to Congress, but she could not satisfy his oversized ego or the equally large sex drive that went with it.

Johnson was a man of immense appetites, and one of them was for women who could fulfill his need for respect and admiration. In 1938 he met Alice Glass. A striking Texas beauty, Glass's background was much like Johnson's, and, like him, she too was determined to be a success. Attracted to politics, she traveled to Austin, the state capital, where she caught the eye of Texas financier Charles Marsh, over twenty years her senior. Glass soon became his mistress, and Marsh took her to Virginia where the two lived together at "Longlea," a picturesque estate not far from Washington.

Longlea had become a gathering place for diplomats, artists, and political figures of the day, and none ever left unimpressed by Glass and her opinions. After a trip with Marsh to Germany, Glass returned to America moved by the plight of European Jews, particularly Jewish artists. Before long, her Virginia home became a way station for musicians, composers, and others fleeing Nazi Germany. When one, a young Jewish conductor, had a problem with his U.S. visa, Marsh called on freshman congressman Lyndon Johnson for help, and in a matter of days the difficulty was resolved.

Glass took note of Johnson's efficiency as well as his compassion. All the Texas politicians she had ever known were crooks. Johnson was different, she thought, and the more she listened to him talk about his impoverished upbringing and his goal of helping people, the more she liked him. She also recognized that Johnson had a lot to learn. She taught him table manners, showed him what kind of clothes to wear, and even read poetry to him.

Within a matter of months Johnson and Glass began meeting in secret when Marsh was out of town. Going to bed with the live-in girlfriend of one of the richest men in Texas could have been political suicide for a less shrewd politician, but Johnson took the situation in stride.

For someone who used to call his penis "Jumbo" and brag about his one-night stands to cronies, Johnson kept uncharacteristically quiet about his affair with Glass. He also went right on treating Marsh as his mentor, a role the older man was more than willing to play. Marsh donated money to Johnson's campaigns and let him in on sure-thing real estate investments. Among the many newspapers Marsh owned was the *Austin American-Statesman,* which, on his instructions, regularly ran articles and editorials favorable to Johnson.

Throughout his early career in Washington, Johnson relied on similar assistance from older benefactors, like Georgia senator Richard Russell. Still, no one provided him with better service than Marsh, who apparently never discovered Johnson's deception.

If Lady Bird guessed something was amiss, she never let on, either. "We were all together a lot—Lyndon and Lady Bird and Charles and Alice," recalled Glass's sister Mary Louise, who knew all about the affair. "Lady Bird never said a word. She showed nothing, nothing at all."

Glass's relationship with Johnson continued into the late 1960s, when the two had a permanent falling-out over the Vietnam War. Glass, who detested the war and Johnson's role in it, abruptly broke off all contact, and they never saw each other again.

Johnson's libido was legendary. And it appeared he only had two daughters, Lynda Bird and Lucy Baines, to show for it until 1987, when a Texas woman, Madeleine Brown, claimed she had an affair with Johnson that produced a son in 1950.

"[Lyndon] looked at me like I was an ice cream cone on a hot day," she told *People* magazine. "He had a certain amount of roughness about him, and maybe that's what I liked."

Brown was no Alice Glass, but her affair with Johnson lasted almost as long—over twenty years. After the child was born, Johnson agreed to buy her a house, Brown said, and pay all her bills through a Dallas attorney.

When Johnson became president, his preoccupation with the war in Vietnam brought a gradual end to their regular meetings, many of which occurred at a hotel in Austin, a short drive from the Johnson ranch.

Brown and Johnson met one final time at Houston's Shamrock Hotel. Brown, who thought Johnson had always seemed "like an iron man," could see that the stress of the war and other problems had taken their toll. "There comes a point in the lives of two people," she said, "when they have to face reality. I think that's what we did."

Brown said they "didn't even try to make love" but instead talked for two hours, then kissed and parted company.

It's Fun to Stay at the YMCA

A month before the 1964 presidential election, Walter Jenkins, a forty-six-year-old White House assistant to Lyndon Johnson, was arrested in the men's room of a Washington YMCA for "disorderly conduct," the term then commonly used by police to describe homosexual activity. It was the second time in five years that Jenkins had been arrested in the same location on the same charge.

Johnson's press secretary, George Reedy, announced that Jenkins, who had turned in his resignation after the story broke, was in a hospital "suffering from fatigue" and "nervous exhaustion."

For Johnson, the Jenkins scandal was the second major crisis of the campaign. The first was the Bobby Baker case. Baker, Johnson's secretary when he was Senate majority leader, was the subject of congressional hearings on charges of fraud and corruption in connection with several large defense contracts. Jenkins, a longtime Johnson lieutenant, was scheduled to be a key hearing witness.

Republican candidate Barry Goldwater charged that

Johnson had rushed Jenkins into the hospital for the same reason he had pressured the Senate to postpone the Baker investigation until after the election. "One man stands in the way of the truth," Goldwater said, "because the truth leads right straight to the White House."

Jenkins was fined $50 for his offense. Baker was later convicted of fraud and sent to prison. Johnson's legal adviser, Abe Fortas, who had helped shield the president from political damage in both cases, was later rewarded for his faithful service with a seat on the Supreme Court, only to be forced to resign when he got caught taking improper speaking fees.

Lyndon Johnson and John Kennedy, who shared a similar interest in female loveliness, eyeball the Mona Lisa as Jacqueline Kennedy turns on the charm. *[U.S. Information Agency]*

LBJ imposes on tiny Texas senator John Tower, later the subject of a congressional probe into his heavy drinking and chronic womanizing. *[U.S. Senate Historical Office]*

In 1964, Johnson aide Walter Jenkins, shown here with Lady Bird's press secretary, Liz Carpenter, was arrested in a Washington men's room. *[Copyright The Washington Post; reprinted by permission of the D.C. Public Library]*

8

Closet Casanova

In 1982, a public opinion poll by Louis Harris showed that 53 percent of those questioned believed that Richard Nixon "set the lowest moral standards" of any of the previous nine presidents. An ABC News survey taken the same year found that by two to one, Americans felt Nixon should be allowed no future role in public affairs.

Apparently, somebody forgot to tell him that. Nixon wrote books, lectured, and advised presidents on foreign affairs right up until his death in 1994.

"The guy had more comebacks than Lazarus," remarked his biographer, Robert Sam Anson. The comebacks presumably have ceased. Just the same, questions about what made Richard Nixon tick are likely to continue for some time.

The resentment that the former president faced after the Watergate scandal might have forced a less driven politician to retire from public life completely. Yet as Nixon himself showed over and over again throughout his career, sticks and stones were his natural element. Speaking at Oxford University in 1978, four years after he resigned the presidency in disgrace, Nixon left little doubt that his complex constitution abhorred a vacuum.

"I'm very comfortable," he said of his exile. "I have enough. I could be content to go out with my wife or sit and contemplate my navel, but if I did that—if I turned my mind off—I would be mentally dead in one year and physically dead in two."

The "old" Nixon cried during his "Checkers" speech in 1952, when he offered to take himself off the Republican ticket after accepting questionable campaign contributions. The post-Watergate Nixon showed no visible signs of remorse.

The first time Nixon's future wife, Pat Ryan, met him she "thought he was nuts." As years went by, she had lots of company.

Richard Nixon is probably the most psychoanalyzed president in U.S. history. Remembered for his weird body language and strange remarks—once, before a TV interview with David Frost, he asked Frost, "Well, did you do any fornicating this weekend?"—it's the neurotic inner Nixon that still fascinates, maybe now more than ever.

Nixon's joyless Depression upbringing is often credited with producing an insecure man starved for love and affection. To many who knew him, Nixon seemed totally uninterested in sex. After seeing him at a political event surrounded by Hollywood actresses, writer Adela Rogers St. John was struck by his odd indifference. "You never saw such beautiful flesh," she said. "And he acted like a man utterly unsexed. It was as if he didn't know they were there."

Despite appearances, Nixon's mysterious private life was not entirely devoid of romance. In 1976, information surfaced about his friendship with a Hong Kong cocktail waitress. The woman, Marianna Liu, a Chinese national, who first met

Nixon in the late 1950s, was later investigated by the FBI as a possible foreign intelligence agent.

Nixon socialized with Liu during three visits to Hong Kong between 1964 and 1966, when she and another waitress met him and his friend, Florida businessman Bebe Rebozo, in a suite at the Mandarin Hotel. On a fourth visit, in 1967, Liu was in the hospital when Nixon arrived, and he sent her flowers and perfume but did not visit her room.

The FBI investigation into Nixon's relationship with Liu started when the bureau's "legal attaché" at the U.S. consulate in Hong Kong wrote a letter on the subject to J. Edgar Hoover. The FBI chief added the material to an already extensive collection of information on Liu in the bureau's so-called obscene matters files, where Hoover kept detailed records on the sex lives of politicians.

The investigation, which lasted from the fall of 1967 to July 1969, six months into Nixon's presidency, reportedly failed to find any evidence that Liu was a threat to national security or that she and Nixon were ever more than friends. However, since all records in the case were sealed, suspicion of an affair, although unproven, has persisted.

In a 1976 interview with the *New York Times,* Liu denied that she and Nixon had ever been intimate and that she sought his help in immigrating to America, but events could easily be interpreted otherwise. Liu was admitted to the United States on December 1, 1969. An FBI source recalled having been told that Nixon somehow "intervened" on her behalf with the Immigration and Naturalization Service. The first place she lived was Whittier, California, Nixon's hometown.

At the time of her interview with the *Times,* Liu refused to sign a release that would make her immigration file public.

Secret Service records show that in 1970 Liu visited the White House on at least two occasions. The following year, however, Nixon apparently ended the relationship, perhaps after talking to Hoover, who had told an aide he planned to "take [the Liu case] up directly with the president," or perhaps, as some have speculated, because his wife, Pat, put an end to their relationship.

Liu remained in the United States, eventually becoming a citizen and settling in the Los Angeles suburbs.

Richard Nixon tests his courage in this 1953 encounter with a lion. *[U.S. Senate Historical Office]*

Elvis Presley, showing the effects of his pill habit, pays a surprise visit to the White House, where Nixon makes him an honorary drug enforcement agent. *[The National Archives, Nixon Project]*

Taking command of a golf cart, Nixon demonstrates his driving skills for wife, Pat, and longtime best buddy, Bebe Rebozo. *[The National Archives, Nixon Project]*

Kitchen staff prepares Nixon's final meal in the White House: pineapple slices, cottage cheese, and a glass of milk. *[The National Archives, Nixon Project]*

RICHARD NIXON'S ENEMIES LIST

Here, in alphabetical order, are the political enemies targeted for IRS audits, wiretaps, and other forms of harassment by the Nixon administration. The original list was first made public by White House legal counsel John Dean in 1973 during the Senate Watergate Hearings.

Alexander E. Barkan, AFL-CIO
Carol Channing, actress
John Conyers, Democratic congressman from
   Michigan
Bill Cosby, comedian
Maxwell Dane, advertising executive
Sidney Davidoff, assistant to former New York
   mayor John V. Lindsay
Ronald Dellums, Democratic congressman from
   California
S. Harrison Dogole, Global Security Systems
Charles Dyson, associate of former Democratic
   National Committee chairman Lawrence
   O'Brien
Bernard T. Feld, Council for a Livable World
Jane Fonda, actress
Edward Guthman, *Los Angeles Times* editor
Morton Halperin, Common Cause
Samuel M. Lambert, National Education Association
Allard Lowenstein, former Democratic congressman
   from New York
Mary McGrory, former *Washington Star* columnist
Stewart R. Mott, liberal philanthropist
S. Sterling Munro Jr., assistant to former Democratic
   senator Henry Jackson of Washington
Paul Newman, actor

Arnold Picker, United Artists Corp.
Tony Randall, actor
Daniel Schorr, former CBS correspondent
Howard Stein, chairman of the Dreyfus Corp.
Leonard Woodcock, United Automobile Workers

ART LOVERS

No man deserved to be a Republican vice president more than Nelson A. Rockefeller, but it would take a chain of events unprecedented in American politics to put him in office.

First, V.P. Spiro Agnew was charged with taking bribes and kickbacks when he was governor of Maryland. Agnew copped a plea on tax evasion and resigned in 1973. Then, Rep. Gerald Ford was named to replace him. After Watergate forced Nixon to quit, Ford became president and named Rockefeller to take over his old job as vice president.

Rocky loved the do-nothing number two post, since it gave him lots of free time to do what he really liked, namely, use his vast fortune to collect rare works of art, many of which he and his wife, Happy, put on display in the new vice president's house.

His favorite piece was a surrealistic bed, which was unveiled with great media fanfare, even as some wondered how Rocky would put it to use.

Megan Marshak was a young assistant press secretary who stayed on Rockefeller's personal staff after the Republicans lost the White House in 1977. It was a career move that would loom large at the time of her boss's demise.

Marshak and Rockefeller were supposedly working on an "art book" one night in January 1979 when the former vice president suffered a fatal heart attack.

Nearly an hour passed before help was summoned, a gap that caused considerable speculation on what the two art lovers had been up to. That speculation was heightened when it was learned that Marshak had been wearing an evening gown on that fatal night and that the seventy-year-old Rockefeller was shoeless.

Rumors suggesting that Rocky had died in the saddle made the rounds before family money and Marshak's resolute public silence defused what could have been an embarrassing posthumous sex scandal.

KISSINGER AND TELL

In 1987, Nixon's former secretary of state, Henry Kissinger, brought a $10 million lawsuit against *Penthouse* magazine for publishing an interview with him. The interview had been given to two freelance writers who sold the story to the highest bidder. Kissinger, a Nobel Peace Prize winner, claimed the interview, which he thought was going to be used as part of a book on foreign policy, had harmed his professional reputation.

During his years in Washington, Kissinger, who had been romantically linked to some of Hollywood's most alluring stars and starlets, had a very different image from the one he sought to promote after leaving government. And in a deposition for his lawsuit, the man widely known as Super K (for his great self-esteem) revealed how touchy he could be on the subject of sex. The *Penthouse* attorney was the late trial lawyer Roy Grutman.

QUESTION: Were you aware that, among other things, *Penthouse* is one of the foremost men's entertainment magazines, and frequently publishes pictures of beautiful nude ladies?

KISSINGER: Of course, I am aware of that.

QUESTION: Have you ever sought to cultivate a public image of yourself as a lothario?

KISSINGER: No.

QUESTION: Are you aware of the fact that you have had a reputation of being something of a ladies' man?

KISSINGER: Certainly, when I was unmarried.

QUESTION: And did you ever do anything to refute that image?

KISSINGER: I did nothing to promote it or refute it.

QUESTION: As a matter of fact, you were married in what year?

KISSINGER: 1974.

QUESTION: I draw your attention to a newspaper article

Henry Kissinger, who coined the phrase "Power is the ultimate aphrodisiac," explains how he got the idea to wife, Nancy, and Nelson Rockefeller. *[Copyright Washington Post; reprinted by permission of the D.C. Public Library]*

that appeared on January 19, 1987, in the *New York Post*, in which you are quoted as saying, "Spread it around that I am sexy, says Henry," speaking of you, originator of the immortal line "Power is the ultimate aphrodisiac." Did you say that?

KISSINGER: If it was quoted, I must have said it.

QUESTION: So, by your public statements and public activities you have not portrayed yourself as being shy in some respects in sexual things?

KISSINGER: Sexual subjects is different. If you are saying— This was, anyway, a joking conversation with the author at the dinner table.

QUESTION: Was that at Café Mortimer?

KISSINGER: Yes, but . . .

A few days later, after considering the effect further questioning along these lines might have on his place in history, Kissinger decided to drop his suit.

9

Car Trouble

At 2:00 A.M. on October 8, 1974, a black-and-silver Lincoln belonging to House Ways and Means chairman Wilbur Mills was stopped by police near the Washington Tidal Basin. Cops had noticed the car weaving suspiciously and decided to investigate. The incident not only marked the beginning of the end of Mills's long political career, it opened a whole new era in the media coverage of congressional drinking habits, a subject previously considered off-limits.

Accompanying Mills were stripper Anabella Battistella, who performed under the stage name of "Fanne Foxe, the Argentine Firecracker," and several of her South American friends. After police intervened, Foxe jumped into the Tidal Basin in what was described as a "suicide attempt," while the other occupants of the car began fighting one another. Only Mills, who was drunk and bleeding from scratches on his face, cooperated with authorities.

Involved at the time in one of the toughest campaigns of

his life, Mills, a sixty-five-year-old Arkansas Democrat, won reelection by telling voters that the Fanne Foxe affair taught him "never to drink champagne with foreigners." What he neglected to mention was that his beverage of choice happened to be vodka, which he was consuming at the rate of two fifths a day.

Following a brief stay in a local hospital for observation, Foxe went back to dancing, and Mills, who was never charged, resumed his congressional duties. Then, two months later, Mills showed up at a Boston burlesque theater where Foxe was the headline attraction, this time billed as the "Tidal Basin Bombshell." Reporters and photographers soon arrived and found Mills in Foxe's dressing room, even drunker than when he was stopped by the police in Washington.

"She has a wonderful act," Mills said, "and if she wants to, I can get her into the movies." The lawmaker claimed to have helped "fourteen or fifteen" other performers reach stardom and said he had created a film script for Foxe called *It's Not Burlesque.* He added that he had also written a screenplay about Richard Nixon.

Asked if showing up at the burlesque theater could hurt him politically, Mills boldly babbled: "This won't ruin me. . . . Nothing can ruin me."

A few days after his appearance in Boston, Mills checked himself into the first of several alcohol rehabilitation clinics, emerging months later to find he had been stripped of the Ways and Means chairmanship. Mills served out the rest of his term in Congress before retiring in 1976 to become a tax consultant.

Fanne Foxe had a brief acting career, landing the lead role in a low-budget movie called *Posse from Heaven,* which closed after playing just one day in Washington.

Since Mills's departure, chairmen of the House Ways and Means Committee have proven to be a particularly endangered species. His successor, Rep. Al Ullman, was voted out of office by angry Oregon voters when they learned he had sold his house in the state and moved to Washington. More recently, Rep. Dan Rostenkowski, the Illinois Democrat, was deposed as chairman and lost reelection after being indicted on multiple counts of criminal wrongdoing and corruption.

"I wouldn't say the job is cursed," said one Capitol Hill reporter, "but it definitely should come with a warning label."

Mills watches Fanne Foxe perform from the wings of a Boston burlesque theater. *[UPI/Bettmann]*

When he ran for president in 1972, Rep. Wilbur Mills (right) was drinking as much as two fifths of vodka a day. *[Copyright The Washington Post; reproduced by permission of the D.C. Public Library]*

10

The
Bimbo Decade

From Watergate to ABSCAM, the 1970s in Washington was a decade defined by scandals. If the Wilbur Mills affair made alcoholism fair game for the media, a series of disgruntled ex-girlfriends soon did the same thing for sex.

First, there was the staffer named "Dorothy," who tape-recorded her get-togethers with then–Michigan representative Don Riegle. The remarkable thing, though, wasn't the sex, but Riegle's ability to talk business with no clothes on.

> RIEGLE: I love you.
> DOROTHY: Don, I love you and I'll always love—
> RIEGLE: And I'll always love you ... I ... I ... God, feel
> such super love for you. By the way, the newsletter
> should start arriving.

Shortly after this particular recording was made, Riegle, a Democrat with a wife and three children, dumped Dorothy, got a divorce, and married another woman who worked in his office. Dorothy, feeling she had been unfairly treated, handed over her tape collection to the *Detroit News,* which published selected portions of the transcripts on the front page. Riegle was embarrassed but went on to serve nearly twenty more years in Congress.

Rep. Wayne Hays, chairman of the House Administration Committee, wasn't so lucky. For years, Hays had a reputation as the meanest man in Congress, so when the story broke, in 1976, that he had been keeping his girlfriend on his office payroll, few, if any, on the Hill felt sorry for him. To make matters worse, the woman in question, an ex–beauty queen named Elizabeth Ray, confessed she couldn't type. In a place famous for paperwork, she kept herself busy doing her nails and reading romance novels. "I can't even answer the phone," said the thirty-three-year-old Ray, who apparently performed well enough in other areas to make herself a valued employee.

Hays's problems began when he married the secretary in his Ohio office and neglected to invite Ray to the wedding. "It's not that I care so much about him getting married," Ray told reporters, "but it looks bad that I'm not invited. I was good enough to be his mistress for two years, but not good enough to be invited to his wedding."

When Ray asked Hays how her job would be affected, he informed her that if she behaved, she would still qualify as "mistress No. 1." A few days later, Ray paid a visit to the *Washington Post.*

At first, Hays denied Ray's charges, saying he had spoken to her psychiatrist and "she's a very sick girl." After the FBI began snooping around, Hays, then sixty-four, admitted having the affair, and in traditional fashion threw himself on the mercy of Congress. "I hope when the time comes to leave this house, which I love," he told fellow lawmakers, "Wayne

Hays may be remembered as mean . . . but I hope Wayne Hays will never be thought of as dishonest."

Ray's hard-luck story lost some of its appeal when she claimed to have been intimate with other big-name Democrats, like former vice president Hubert Humphrey, before working her way to Hays.

"I'll handle this," House Speaker Carl Albert said of the scandal. But in no time Albert had his own mess to contend with. His private Hill office was named by Ray as the scene of regular congressional orgies attended by her and other women. Albert denied the accusations.

"I haven't been to bed with a girl this year," protested Albert. "I'm sixty-eight." The next day he announced his "irreversible" decision to retire from Congress.

Hays tried to commit suicide by taking an overdose of sleeping pills. By the time he recovered, his career in Congress was over, and he resigned.

Ray, whose lack of office skills had made headlines, left town to take up acting in dinner theater, but not before appearing in *Playboy* and publishing a novel called *The Washington Fringe Benefit*.

"I just liked Hays for his power," she said several years later, "and because he was the sharpest dresser I ever saw."

ABSCAM was the code name for a 1980 FBI sting operation that eventually netted seven members of Congress. Never before had the voting public been given the opportunity to see and hear so many elected officials breaking the law on live-action videotape. The culprits, Sen. Harrison Williams of New Jersey and Reps. John Jenrette of South Carolina, John Murphy of New York, Frank Thompson of New Jersey, Raymond Lederer and Michael Myers of Pennsylvania, and Richard Kelly of Florida, the lone Republican, were all found guilty of accepting bribes.

Only one potential sting victim, Republican senator Larry Pressler of South Dakota, failed to take the bait. When he was offered $50,000 in exchange for helping to get a "wealthy Arab" into the country, Pressler replied, "What you are suggesting may be illegal," and turned down the proposal.

All the sting victims were convicted and sentenced to prison. Before he did time, one member of the group, Raymond Lederer, was actually reelected.

Some critics charged the FBI with entrapment. Even so, it was hard to overlook how eagerly the targeted lawmakers went along with the scheme. Jenrette, who blamed his moral lapse on a drinking problem, seemed to sum up the motives of the sleazy seven when he boasted to one undercover agent that he had "larceny" in his heart.

He also had a lot of money in his shoes, where his attractive wife, Rita, found $250,000 in bribes that Jenrette received from the ex-convict who played the role of the sheikh for the FBI.

ABSCAM may have been the biggest Democratic money scandal of the century, but Rita Jenrette soon took center stage.

Like Liz Ray, she too appeared nude in *Playboy,* where she revealed among other things that she and Jenrette had sex on the Capitol steps. And while she was promoting the magazine on *The Phil Donahue Show,* who should call in but her estranged husband. "I want to make one thing very clear," Jenrette said on the air. "I never wanted Rita to pose for *Playboy.* I begged her not to."

"That's not true," answered his wife, who had said earlier on the program that her husband encouraged her to pose for *Playboy* to help pay his legal bills.

"Off the booze?" Donahue inquired of Jenrette.

"Oh, yeah," assured the former congressman.

*   *   *

Perhaps the most accomplished femme fatale of her era, Paula Parkinson, demonstrated that you don't have to be a man to make it as a Washington lobbyist. Between 1978 and 1981 Parkinson had congressmen lining up to see her. In her unstinting promotion of agricultural insurance, the shapely influence peddler claimed to have had sex with eight different members of Congress, all but one of them Republicans.

Parkinson was accused of trading sex for votes, a charge the FBI could never prove, though rumors persist that the bureau has in its possession videotapes of Parkinson and some of her Capitol Hill partners in very embarrassing positions. She also helped to end the careers of two members of Congress who accompanied her on the most notorious golf trip in American politics.

The 1980 outing included three Republican congressmen: Tom Evans of Delaware, Tom Railsback of Illinois, and Dan Quayle of Indiana. In addition, a half-dozen male lobbyists came along. Evans, married and the father of three, had been dating Parkinson for several months before the trip, but denied their relationship involved politics, which would have violated House ethics. Even when the vote was on agricultural insurance, Evans declared, the only thing that influenced him was "my economic philosophy."

On the golf trip, Evans and Parkinson slept in the same hotel room. The other congressmen shared rooms with lobbyists. When the scandal hit, Quayle called a press conference to announce that he had roomed with lobbyist William Hecht.

"I guess you might want to make something homosexual out of it," he said to reporters.

Evans and Railsback both lost their next elections. Quayle, who survived and moved up to the Senate, was chosen in 1988 to run for vice president on the GOP ticket with George Bush. During the campaign, the notorious golf trip was back in the news. So was Parkinson. Bearing little resemblance to the legislative lovely she had once been, a plumper Paula taped a preelection *Geraldo Rivera* show, telling how Quayle had tried unsuccessfully to pick her up. She also recounted tales about other randy Republicans, but the program never aired, and Parkinson returned to Dallas and her job of selling decorative plumbing fixtures.

THE KEATING FIVE

There are an estimated 149 lobbyists in Washington for every member of Congress. But it isn't the lobbyists who are chasing the lawmakers. It's the lawmakers who are usually chasing them. Without cash contributions from special interests, most senators and representatives could never raise the $20,000 they need to take in every week to pay for their reelection campaigns.

Congress makes laws, and generous donors, through the use of applied capital, make sure the politicians in charge keep their friends in mind.

That's what happened when savings-and-loan swindler Charles Keating asked five senators to intervene on his behalf with federal bank regulators. Alan Cranston of California, Don Riegle of Michigan (and the "Dorothy" tapes), Dennis DeConcini of Arizona, John Glenn of Ohio, and John McCain of Arizona, the only Republican, all saw good reason to help someone in Keating's position.

The only problem was that Keating had bilked his depositors of millions of dollars, and when branches of his Lincoln Savings and Loan started folding, the political fallout was lethal.

The bad publicity forced Riegle, DeConcini, and Cranston, the sole member of the five to get an official reprimand, all to retire when their terms expired. The case also established "the appearance of impropriety" as a new offense in Senate ethics.

Sen. Don Riegle's girlfriend tape-recorded the highlights of their office romance when he was a congressman. *[Roll Call]*

Liz Ray earned $14,000 a year working as an in-House mistress for Rep. Wayne Hays. *[Roll Call]*

Henry Kissinger says a few kind words for Hays (left), who bows his head in contemplation. *[U.S. House of Representatives]*

Rita Jenrette found $250,000 in bribe money hidden in her husband's shoes. *[U.S. House of Representatives]*

11

Staff Infection

In 1983, Jim Bates, a freshman congressman from San Diego, arrived in Washington. Bates, a brash Democrat, soon developed a reputation for being one of the worst bosses on Capitol Hill, and considering that members of Congress regularly treat their employees like full-time servants, that's no easy achievement.

Hill staffers not only work hard, they're also on display. When asked why he only hired former beauty queens to be secretaries in his Capitol Hill office, Texas representative Charles Wilson replied, "You can always teach 'em to type, but you can't teach 'em to grow tits."

Members of Congress, like politicians everywhere, need constant care, and the people who often provide it are their office staffs. The bond that results can be intensely personal, so personal at times it's romantic. But in politics there's a thin line between attraction and repulsion. Many staffers would do anything for their senators or representatives, up to and including marry them, while others fear they might accidentally turn their bosses on.

Jim Bates had a lot of competition when it came to annoying his female staffers, but few members of Congress have been more consistently obnoxious. During his eight years in office, Bates thrived on a regular routine of grabbing attractive secretaries and hugging them, as he put it, to give himself "more energy." He asked them to sleep with him and commented on their breast size and rear ends. One woman in his office revealed how he liked to attach himself to her leg, which he would straddle as they discussed legislative business. And that wasn't the only way the congressman wanted to get physical. Another female on his staff told a reporter that Bates informed her he often thought about hitting an office assistant "until blood trickled from her mouth."

For years, no one complained, fearing that if they did, their careers on the Hill would be ruined. Then in 1987, two women, who couldn't take it anymore, filed charges against Bates with the House Ethics Committee. The panel's mild response surprised no one. After hearing the case, committee members sent Bates a letter asking him to apologize to the women.

"I think I made a mistake," said Bates. "I didn't really know what sexual harassment was."

But his constituents clearly did. When Bates's behavior made news back in San Diego, he was voted out of office.

One woman in his office complained that Rep. Jim Bates had the annoying habit of attaching himself to her leg. *[Roll Call]*

12

Method Acting

By the time Ronald Reagan moved into the White House he could outperform most politicians half his age. A thirty-year career in movies and television was perfect training for his new job. Which explains why he delegated all the hard work to aides and assistants. In the wake of Jimmy Carter's no-frills presidency, the country was ready for some show business, and that's exactly what the new chief executive provided.

Ronald and Nancy Reagan expanded the concept of First Family to include hairdressers, fashion consultants, and interior designers, not to mention a whole cast of vintage film stars and entertainers. Commenting on one early Reagan party, comedian Mark Russell said the guest list reminded him of "open house at the Hollywood Wax Museum."

It didn't take the Reagans long to turn Washington into Beverly Hills East. No sooner had Nancy unpacked her Adolfo dresses than she started redoing the executive mansion to look like a set from a high-budget costume epic. Her critics called her "Queen Nancy," and when her imperial style became a political issue, the White House took the Hollywood approach to changing her image. In a brilliant piece of countercasting, Nancy, mustering all of her acting skills, showed up at an annual banquet for reporters dressed in a boa and rags to sing "Second Hand Rose." The media approved, and the bad press stopped, at least for the time being.

If the entertainment industry loved Ron and Nancy, there were those in Hollywood who saw them in a different light. The Reagans supported the platform of the religious right, but their past lives in Movieland were, by some accounts, hardly shining examples of high morality. In a biography of Peter Lawford, author Patricia Seaton Lawford, the late actor's wife, recalls this Nancy Reagan story:

"I can remember when Peter was watching the news right after Reagan was elected. He went over to the set, laughing and calling Mrs. Reagan a vulgar name. I was shocked and wanted to know what was bothering him. He laughed again and said that when she was single, Nancy Davis was known for giving the best head in Hollywood.

"Then Peter told of driving to the Phoenix area with Nancy Davis and Bob Walker [a minor movie star in the 1940s]. Nancy would visit her parents, Dr. and Mrs. Loyal Davis, while Peter and Walker picked up girls at Arizona State University in Tempe, a Phoenix suburb. He claimed that she entertained them orally on those trips, apparently playing with whichever man was not driving."

Both Reagans owe their public personalities in large part to Hollywood hype. If Nancy was typecast in her limited screen roles as the girl next door, Ron was a grown-up version of the all-American boy.

In a ghostwritten article for *Photoplay* magazine in 1942, entitled "How to Make Yourself Important," Reagan offered this revealing and, in some ways, prophetic self-analysis:

Method Acting

"Mr. Norm is my alias, or shouldn't I admit it," he began, evincing the same down-to-earth quality voters would later find so appealing. "I'm interested in politics and government," he added, confessing that when he first came to Hollywood, "All I had in this world was the confidence that, with the proper material, I could entertain people."

Reagan continued: "For me, the one job in the world I want to do is acting." But World War II changed that, and Reagan put on a uniform to act in Army training films. "Who knows?" concluded the future president. "Maybe when [the war is over] there will be other good parts for me."

As things worked out, none were as good as the ones he would get to play in politics.

Reagan became head of the Screen Actors Guild in 1947. He met Nancy when she sought his advice on how to get her name removed from a list of Hollywood communists. As it turned out, the name belonged to another Nancy Davis. The incident, however, helped form one of the most ambitious political partnerships in American history.

With his career in decline, Reagan's five years as SAG president showed him he could do far better working for the people behind the camera than he ever could in front of it.

Under Reagan's leadership the guild voted to waive the normal rules and allow the Music Corporation of America, which also happened to be *his* talent agency, to become a full-fledged production company, effectively letting it reap the rewards of packaging motion pictures from start to finish.

In 1962, Reagan was subpoenaed to testify before a federal grand jury investigating kickbacks that he may have received from MCA for helping it become a billion-dollar entertainment conglomerate. If the allegations of illegal payoffs could never be proved, it's clear that Reagan's financial situation improved right along with MCA's. Following the waiver, real estate deals, television shows, and Las Vegas nightclub appearances, all involving MCA, made Ronald Reagan a wealthy man.

In 1960, Reagan returned briefly to head the union during a bitter actors' strike and proceeded to negotiate a "sweetheart" settlement with the studios. According to author Dan E. Moldea, "People in Hollywood still refer to it as the big giveaway."

Four years later, Reagan made a speech supporting conservative Barry Goldwater for president. Goldwater lost the election; however, Reagan's speech propelled him into a political career that took him all the way to Washington, where he ran the country using the same skills he learned in Hollywood.

Not since the days of Ulysses S. Grant had a president brought more of his cronies into government. Personal friends and business associates were given cabinet posts. Longtime aides were made top advisers. The Reagan administration was thick with opportunists, many of whom, not surprisingly, got into trouble.

Attorney General Edwin Meese was investigated for helping a bogus defense firm in the Bronx called Wedtech secure Pentagon contracts. Former White House assistant Michael Deaver was convicted of perjury in connection with ethics violations after leaving the government to become a lobbyist. HUD secretary Samuel Pierce was the subject of congressional hearings into a billion-dollar public housing scam. Others, including John Poindexter and marine colonel Oliver North, were forced out of their White House jobs by the Iran-contra scandal, a scheme to raise funds for fighting the communists in Central America by illegally selling arms to the Iranian government.

Reagan also suffered the embarrassment of being the first president to have a Supreme Court nominee, Judge Douglas Ginsburg, withdraw from consideration because of drug use.

Nancy was even accused of having a White House affair with Frank Sinatra. What the president knew and when he knew it became *the* Washington mystery question of the 1980s.

Method Acting

Reagan left town the same genial guy he was when he first arrived. During the eight years in between, however, over two hundred of his appointees faced allegations of ethical and criminal misconduct. History will write the final review. But one conclusion seems unavoidably clear. In his greatest role ever, Ronald Reagan was upstaged by too many bad actors.

Ronald Reagan and fellow actor-turned-politician George Murphy discuss world affairs. Publicity photo shows Reagan as host of TV's *Death Valley Days.* *[U.S. Senate Historical Office]*

Reagan appears on Capitol Hill with wife, Nancy. What strange power did she hold over some of Hollywood's best-known actors? *[U.S. Senate Historical Office]*

Iran-contra pinup Fawn Hall has a laugh with celebrity interviewer Larry King. Once Oliver North's secretary, Hall ended up in drug rehab. *[Roll Call]*

13

Monkey Business

No Washington politician since John F. Kennedy has led a more daring private life than Sen. Gary Hart. Described by both friends and opponents as "self-destructive," the Colorado Democrat can take credit for making the label of "womanizer" the political kiss of death it is today.

Hart once told an inquiring reporter, "Let's just say I believe in reform marriage." His behavior during two successive presidential races made that abundantly clear. Catching Hart "in the act" became a journalistic obsession. During the 1984 campaign, a producer for NBC News saw him leaving a woman's apartment late one night. But network executives rejected the producer's idea of arranging a video stakeout, since Hart had already lost the nomination to Walter Mondale.

On his next try for the White House, the media went after Hart almost from the day he announced his candidacy on April 13, 1987. As reporters got more demanding, Hart boldly invited them to follow him around.

"I'm serious," he said. "Anyone who wants to put a tail on me, go ahead. They'd be very bored."

That challenge was all the justification newspapers needed. Suddenly, every motel stop on the campaign trail was a potential exposé. A month into the race, the *Miami Herald* received a telephone tip from a woman that Hart was spending the weekend at his house in Washington with a twenty-nine-year-old model named Donna Rice. Hart's wife, Lee, was out of town. In what would become the most famous media surveillance in American politics, *Herald* reporters, for nearly a day, hid behind bushes in Hart's yard, waiting for him and Rice to come outside.

Criticism that the press had gone too far did nothing to stop the seller's market in Gary Hart and Donna Rice stories. With Rice in seclusion and Hart desperately trying to salvage his campaign, associates of both began cashing in on the bonanza. Rice's friend Lynn Armandt proved the most resourceful, earning a reported $100,000 for an account of the couple's trip to Bimini on the aptly named yacht *Monkey Business.*

Meanwhile, evidence emerged of other Hart affairs. After the *Herald* broke the story of Hart's weekend with Donna Rice, the *Washington Post* received information from a detective indicating that the woman whose apartment Hart had been seen leaving in 1984 was actually a longtime girlfriend. The detective had been hired by a former Democratic senator who suspected that Hart might be seeing his wife. No proof of that affair was discovered, but the detective's report on Hart and his old flame would eventually end his campaign.

During a press conference following the *Herald* story, Hart was asked if he had ever committed adultery. That started an unprecedented media feeding frenzy. No information pertaining to the candidate's personal life was off-limits. While Hart attacked the press for invading his privacy, *Post* editors, who confirmed information in the detective's findings, let it be known that they were preparing another story on the senator's sex life.

"If it doesn't bother me, I don't think it ought to bother anyone else," said Hart's wife in defense of her husband's behavior. Yet given the prospect of more sensational sex stories, Hart soon had no choice but to pull out of the race. "Under present circumstances, this campaign cannot go on," he said. "I've made some mistakes. . . . Maybe big mistakes, but not bad mistakes."

The *Post* article was never published, lending credibility to speculation that the paper had negotiated Hart's withdrawal. Not since Watergate had the press been so aggressive in its pursuit of a politician.

Roger Ailes, communication director for George Bush's 1988 campaign, thought Hart's treatment was especially unfair. "Who the hell cares," he said. ". . . Ben Franklin was doing it. Thomas Jefferson was probably doing it too."

And Bush could have also been doing it. An affair Bush was supposedly having with a Capitol Hill secretary (said to have "served under him in a number of positions") had been rumored for years. But in 1988, the big story was Gary Hart's love life, not George Bush's.

After Hart's withdrawal, some papers seemed determined to play vice squad. The *New York Times* sent questionnaires to the fourteen remaining candidates in the race, asking them to provide information ranging from medical records to college transcripts. The request, which was widely criticized and eventually scrapped, also asked candidates to answer questions about their sex lives, including this mantra of the 1988 campaign: "Have you ever committed adultery?"

Gary Hart signs autographs days before a sex scandal ends his political career. *[Roll Call]*

Donna Rice, Hart's girlfriend, appears with Dr. James Sehn, the surgeon who reattached John Wayne Bobbitt's penis *[Bill Thomas]*

The Capitol Hill town house where the press caught Hart and Rice in 1987. *[Roll Call]*

PROFILES IN CHARISMA

"Why do you imitate John Kennedy so much?" CBS news-man Roger Mudd asked Gary Hart. Hart said he didn't imitate Kennedy. What about the haircut and the gestures? Mudd insisted. He hadn't noticed any similarity, Hart replied. Just the same, to millions of American voters the facts spoke for themselves. Gary Hart not only looked like Kennedy, he acted and talked like him too.

But he wasn't the only Washington politician pretending to be John F. Kennedy in the early 1980s, when Kennedy-like qualities helped to elect Democrats and Republicans across the country. Take Massachusetts senator John F. Kerry (note the initials), whose "lantern-jawed ethnic face . . . few Irish Catholic voters can mistake," according to *Congressional Quarterly.* Or former Rep. Jim Slattery from Kansas. "His boyish good looks earn him comparisons to [John] Kennedy," reported *Politics in America,* "and his engaging manner puts to rest the initial impression given by his ice-blue eyes."

It was "impossible to underestimate the political importance of looking like a Kennedy," observed the *Washington Weekly,* citing as a prime example of the trend none other than an up-and-coming congressman from Georgia, Newt Gingrich.

Rep. Jim Slattery. *[U.S. House of Representatives]*

Sen. Max Baucus. *[U.S. House of Representatives]*

Sen. Tim Wirth. *[U.S. House of Representatives]*

Sen. John F. Kerry. *[Roll Call]*

Rep. Jack McKernan. *[U.S. House of Representatives]*

Rep. Newt Gingrich. *[U.S. House of Representatives]*

14

The Beefcake Caucus

In 1989, federal funding for a traveling exhibit of homo-erotic photographs by Robert Mapplethorpe sparked a series of angry confrontations between liberals and conservatives in Congress. South Carolina Republican senator Jesse Helms led the attack by threatening to cut off all government support for the arts unless the Mapplethorpe show was closed down.

In the House, Rep. William Dannemeyer from California said he wasn't just worried about the art exhibits but their long-term moral implications. "Let's not kid ourselves," he declared. "Pornography and homosexuality are not . . . the cause of decline. They are the symptoms of moral decay in a society that has lost its standards."

Dannemeyer quickly made a name for himself as unofficial spokesman for the antigay faction in the House, a role he often used to denounce homosexuality in floor speeches. Once he even put into the *Congressional Record* quotes from a book on gay lovemaking techniques, claiming it was the public's right to know what "homosexuals do."

The passages described orgies and "other activities peculiar to homosexuality such as . . . inserting dildos, certain vegetables and light bulbs . . ." into areas not usually mentioned in government publications.

Dannemeyer's chief foes were Democratic congressmen Barney Frank and Gerry Studds from Massachusetts, the only two openly gay members of Congress. Both Frank and Studds exited the closet in front-page sex scandals that could have ended their careers, but they skillfully survived and became leading spokesmen in the House for gay rights.

In 1983, Studds was caught having sex with a seventeen-year-old male congressional page. Refusing to beg forgiveness, the popular liberal took the direct approach, challenging the definition of sexual wrongdoing. "I do not believe that a relationship which was mutual and voluntary, without coercion [and] without preferential treatment expressed or . . . implied, constitutes improper sexual misconduct," he told his colleagues.

The tactic worked, and following a House censure, Studds resumed his duties. At the same time, another lawmaker, conservative GOP representative Dan Crane from Illinois, who had admitted having sex with a female page, got little support in his district and resigned in disgrace.

One result of the Studds-Crane scandal was a complete revamping of the rules under which the Hill's hundred or so pages live, work, and most of all play. A strict nighttime curfew was put into effect and, to keep the youngsters safe from lecherous lawmakers, a new Congress-proof page dorm was opened.

If Studds's behavior had embarrassed the Democrats, the Barney Frank affair, in 1989, put them in a state of political shock. After the *Washington Times* revealed that a male prostitute, Steve Gobie, was doing business out of Frank's Capitol

Hill apartment, the usually abrasive Harvard-trained lawyer blamed his predicament on bad judgment and loneliness. He met Gobie through an ad in a gay newspaper.

"I was a loser," Frank told a Boston press conference the day after the story appeared, exposing his two-year liaison with Gobie. "I thought I was Henry Higgins," he explained, comparing what he claimed were his efforts to reform Gobie, whose criminal record included felony convictions for selling cocaine and corrupting a minor, to those of the professor in *My Fair Lady* who transformed a young cockney girl into the toast of London society. Frank employed Gobie, whose only discernable talent was selling sex, as his chauffeur, personal aide, and "houseboy."

Liberal columnist Mark Shields suggested it was time for Frank to quit Congress. Norman Ornstein of the American Enterprise Institute, perhaps the most quoted person in Washington, said: "The more Frank is in the news, the more he hurts the Democratic Party because the American public already believes the Democrats are out of sync with the rest of the nation."

The *Boston Globe,* which had always endorsed him, called on Frank to resign from Congress for his own good and the good of his constituents." But Frank refused to go.

Instead, he sent a letter of apology to supporters in his home district, admitting that "what I did was wrong, but it did not affect my public decisions or any public business." Frank told *Newsweek* it was easy for Gobie to "con" him because as a gay member of Congress he had been deprived of "any kind of healthy emotional life." In a ploy later used by Sen. Robert Packwood to ward off his accusers in a sexual harassment case against him, Frank also dropped a hint that Gobie's Capitol Hill prostitution service may have had members of Congress among its clientele.

"I don't know who he's going to say was in my kitchen," Frank said. "I'm vulnerable and other people are vulnerable."

The Beefcake Caucus

While Frank psychoanalyzed his relationship with Gobie, many Democrats supported him publicly, praising his hard work, dedication, and candor. Some liberal House members even defended him on the floor, an obvious contrast to the cold shoulder GOP conservatives gave to Ohio Republican representative Donald "Buz" Lukens after he was arrested in Columbus for having sex with a female teenager.

The difference in treatment had less to do with degrees of moral turpitude than the new code of political correctness. Lukens and other straight lawmakers caught in the act were seen as dirty old men, whereas Studds and Frank were seen as victims.

For eight months, the twelve-member House Ethics Committee was split along party lines over Frank's punishment. Should he be given a mild reprimand or a much harsher censure? Finally the committee recommended a reprimand based on two transgressions, neither of which involved sex. Frank, they decided, had fixed parking tickets for Gobie and

KISS OFF

After news reports in 1994 that Barney Frank and Gerry Studds were spotted kissing at a White House lawn party, an outraged Frank made the following letter public to set the record straight:

"I did not kiss Gerry Studds or his lover at the White House. . . . Congressman Studds and his lover were seated at a picnic table at which Senator [Jesse] Helms joined them, and Herb [Frank's lover] and I did walk over and talk with some of the people at the table. At no point was there any physical contact between myself and Congressman Studds, his lover, or Senator Helms, for that matter."

had written letters to Gobie's parole officer on congressional stationery. After the full House voted to accept the Ethics Committee's recommendations, Frank was officially decloseted. So much so that he and his new lover, Herb Moses, were later welcomed guests of Bill and Hillary Clinton. Moses even bragged to reporters that the two had made history as the first men to dance together at the White House.

Rep. Gerry Studds and friend make merry with former House Speaker Tom Foley. *[Roll Call]*

Washington watched as Rep. Barney Frank changed from doughboy to toy boy.
[Roll Call]

Frank and current love interest, Herb Moses, made history as the first male couple to dance at the White House. *[Roll Call]*

15

Father of
Yeller Journalism

In a town where politics blends comfortably with political punditry, few people have benefited more from the resulting confusion than John McLaughlin. Ex-priest, ex-politician, and current TV talk-show host, McLaughlin has made a career out of career moves.

As editor of the Jesuit weekly *America* in the 1960s, McLaughlin first made a name for himself on the Catholic college lecture circuit, where his speeches on sex had titles like "Intimacy Before Marriage: The Swedish Experience." But it was his conservative political views that attracted Republican officials, who persuaded him to run for the Senate from Rhode Island in 1970. Although he lost the race by a two-to-one margin, his rhetorical skills were noted in Washington, and he was summoned to work as a speechwriter for Richard Nixon.

No typical man of the cloth, McLaughlin was soon earning $30,000 a year, living in a swank apartment, and being seen around town with the same attractive brunette who had managed his Senate campaign. The press dubbed him "Padre Playboy."

McLaughlin adapted easily to life in the besieged administration. When Watergate erupted, he jumped to his boss's defense, calling Nixon "one of the greatest moral leaders of this century." He claimed that the president's use of profanity on the infamous White House tapes was "a form of emotional drainage," and went on to condemn those offended by Nixon's language for their "hypocrisy and self-righteousness which is particularly odious in terms of our Judeo-Christian heritage."

Even Nixon aides who found McLaughlin insufferable had to admit that having a priest on staff did have its advantages. In fact, McLaughlin liked working at the White House so much that Gerald Ford's advisers practically had to drag him out the front door to get rid of him.

Undaunted by the stigma attached to ex-Nixonites, McLaughlin opened a consulting firm. As a priest, he could offer clients special counseling not normally available from the competition. Yet he also faced a personal dilemma posed by his vows of poverty, chastity, and obedience.

His lifestyle, he explained, "is designed to reflect more emphatically the absolute separation of church and state." The Vatican, which he had asked to free him from his promise to remain celibate, disagreed. McLaughlin was formally defrocked, and within a week he married longtime companion Ann Dore.

While his wife's career in government blossomed, culminating with her being named secretary of labor by Ronald Reagan, McLaughlin maneuvered his way up the media ladder from low-wattage radio talk shows to a brand new kind of television public affairs program. The TV networks, he believed, treated Washington too politely. The show he had in mind would be an on-air version of the Spanish Inquisition, with him lording it over a revolving group of regulars as they ranted and raved about politics and politicians.

On the strength of financial backing from a wealthy fellow Nixon alumnus, Richard Moore, who later became ambassador to Ireland, *The McLaughlin Group* was launched in 1982. More like group therapy than the kind of discussion shows people were used to seeing, it didn't take long for the *Group* to make McLaughlin's name synonymous with "yeller" journalism.

The program's original panel consisted of syndicated columnist Robert Novak, Jack Germond of the *Baltimore Sun,* Judith Miller of the *New York Times,* and Chuck Stone of the *Philadelphia Inquirer.* By the time Miller and Stone were replaced by columnists Patrick Buchanan and Morton Kondracke, the *Group* was being blamed for turning news analysis into show business and reducing reasoned debate into a screaming contest.

Meanwhile, McLaughlin was fast becoming the toast of right-wing Washington. At a party celebrating the show's third anniversary, Ronald Reagan himself showed up to offer congratulations.

All was not well on the set, however, where the host was developing a reputation for being a petty tyrant. McLaughlin naturally saw himself as the show's center of attention, but as jockeying for position among the several regulars intensified, he sensed his central role was threatened. The solution was an application of old-fashioned discipline, and when a word count of program transcripts reportedly revealed that Robert Novak, whom McLaughlin had dubbed "the Prince of Darkness," was hogging the mike, the syndicated columnist was banished. Others quickly got the message, and Father John was once again the top talker. "Power as an experience is as intense as sex," McLaughlin once told a reporter. "Power is more pervasive and unremitting. Sex has periods of remission."

In 1988, a lawsuit against him for sexual harassment seemed to suggest that McLaughlin's own "periods of remission" were well below the norm. The $4 million suit, brought by Linda Dean, a former executive assistant at McLaughlin's production company, alleged that she was fired for "her protests ... of sexual harassment toward herself and other women . . . in the office" who were subjected to McLaughlin's "sexually degrading and offensive remarks and behavior."

In her complaint, Dean claimed that McLaughlin had told her he "needed a lot of sex." She also said McLaughlin had touched her "intimately and against her will." The suit contended that another female employee said McLaughlin harassed her too. McLaughlin denied the charges, but the allegations had many in Washington formulating their own theories about power and sex. Others, offended by McLaughlin's past political associations, figured he had gotten what he deserved.

Coming three years before Anita Hill's charges that Supreme Court nominee Clarence Thomas had sexually harassed her by talking about dirty movies, Dean's suit against McLaughlin helped redefine what a Washington sex scandal was. No longer was having sex an absolute requirement to charge wrongdoing. One of the offenses allegedly committed by Thomas was making reference to a pubic hair on a can of Coke.

Critics have called the lynch-mob mentality created by harassment complaints "sexual McCarthyism." Watching Clarence Thomas's treatment, for some, was like watching reruns of communist witch hunts in the 1950s. But it was the case against McLaughlin that paved the way. That the defendant was a journalist, even if by some standards not a real one, made it that much more interesting, since journalists would play a major role in elevating harassment to major-issue status.

Father of Yeller Journalism

Five months after it was filed, Dean's complaint was settled out of court. All records were sealed, a gag order imposed, and for the first time in anyone's memory, John McLaughlin had no comment.

Talk-show host John McLaughlin, a former Jesuit priest, wanted to be released from his vow of chastity so his life might "reflect more emphatically the absolute separation of church and state." *[Roll Call]*

HE SAID . . . SHE SAID

Capitol Hill had never seen anything quite like it. In 1991, the Senate Judiciary Committee was reviewing the nomination of Clarence Thomas, only the second black in history selected to serve on the U.S. Supreme Court, when information surfaced that suggested Thomas was a sexual pervert, addicted to pornography and talking dirty to women.

According to testimony before the committee by law professor Anita Hill, also black, Thomas had repeatedly pestered her for dates while the two worked together in a series of federal agencies. The harassment, Hill claimed, had gone on for years, although it didn't stop her from following Thomas, her boss, from job to job in the government.

Thomas denied the charges, and his defenders described him as a model citizen. But for millions who watched coverage of the confirmation hearings on network television, he will always be remembered as the man who once rented a XXX porno flick called *The Adventures of Black Mama Jama.*

Despite the demand from feminist groups that Thomas be denied a seat on the Court, the full Senate narrowly approved his nomination. Meanwhile, Hill's testimony made her the heroine of a nationwide campaign against sexual harassment.

Clarence Thomas, who now sits on the Supreme Court, defends himself against charges that he watched porno movies and told dirty jokes. *[Roll Call]*

Anita Hill accused Thomas of trying for ten years to get a date with her. *[Roll Call]*

The Senate Judiciary Committee hears testimony against Thomas. Conspicuous by his silence was Sen. Ted Kennedy (second from left). *[Roll Call]*

TALKING HEADS: NEWS MEDIA CELEBRITIES AND THEIR SPEAKING FEES*

$30,000

Diane Sawyer (ABC)
Sam Donaldson (ABC)

$20,000

Cokie Roberts (ABC)
William Safire (*New York Times*)

$18,000

David Brinkley (ABC)

$12,000

George Will (ABC, columnist)

$10,000

Tim Russert (NBC)

$7,500

Judy Woodruff (PBS)
Lisa Meyers (NBC)

$5,000

Fred Barnes (*The Standard*)
Margaret Carlson (*Time*)
Eleanor Clift (*Newsweek*)
Howard Fineman (*Newsweek*)
Jack Germond (*The Baltimore Sun*)
Alan Murray (*The Wall Street Journal*)
Tim O'Brien (ABC)
Ray Suarez (NPR)

* Fees reflect 1995 prices.

16

Giving Good Face

Appearances on TV political talk shows, like *The McLaughlin Group, Meet the Press,* and *Nightline,* can boost a journalist's career in many lucrative ways, which explains the fierce competition for airtime. The shows pay little or nothing, but being seen on them often leads directly to the corporate lecture circuit, network consulting, and, for the lucky few, Hollywood.

Nina Totenberg, the National Public Radio reporter who broke the Clarence Thomas sexual harassment story, played herself in the film *Dave.* Michael Kinsley of *The New Republic* and CNN's *Crossfire* portrayed a nerdy talk-show host in the Japan-bashing action picture *Rising Sun.* Richard Cohen of the *Washington Post,* Clarence Page of the *Chicago Tribune,* and many others have appeared in movies, pretending to be what they are in real life. But *American Spectator* columnist Ben Stein outdid them all. The son of Nixon administration economic adviser Herbert Stein, he followed his star to a whole new career. Stein, who identifies himself at the end of his columns as "a writer and actor in Los Angeles," has landed parts in *Honeymoon in Vegas* and *The Mask.*

At the same time Washington media personalities are crossing the line into show business, an increasing number of show business celebrities are coming to Washington to push their favorite causes and pick up some extra exposure in the process.

David Letterman, Morgan Fairchild, Bruce Willis, Jessica Lange, Woody Allen, Oprah Winfrey, Diana Ross, Michael Jackson, Glenn Close, Tom Cruise, and James Brown are just part of the cast of characters that shows up every year to tell lawmakers what they think about the great issues of the day.

In 1992, TV star Arsenio Hall came to Congress to talk about gang violence. "Violence in this country is destroying the lives of our children and endangering our very future," Hall declared. "The next Colin Powell might not live to adulthood."

This was a sobering thought, especially to Rep. Bill Young, a Florida Republican, who thanked Hall for his thought-provoking testimony by saying, "I'm down with you, bro'."

"That means I'm on your side," Hall said, translating Young's comment for the less funky, as Young, who is white, turned as red as Hall's ruby earring.

Is Arsenio thinking about a career in politics now that his talk show is off the air?

If so, he may want to look to new Republican representative Sonny Bono of California as a role model. Bono, who used to be half of the singing duo Sonny and Cher, was part of the 1994 GOP landslide. Once, Bono appeared on the Hill as concerned star. Now look at him.

"Can you believe it?" he said, arriving in Washington. "I'm a congressman!"

But his ex-wife, Cher, wasn't surprised.

"Politicians are one step below used-car salesmen," she said. "Sonny should be right at home."

Steven Spielberg against
hate crimes. *[Roll Call]*

Charlton Heston for workers'
rights. *[Roll Call]*

Jessica Lange for Romanian orphans. *[Roll Call]*

Whoopi Goldberg and Robin Williams for the homeless. *[Roll Call]*

Ted Danson against ocean dumping. *[Roll Call]*

Arsenio Hall against gang violence. *[Roll Call]*

17

La Crème
de la Compost

If Jack Kent Cooke weren't one of the richest men in America, he might be just another dirty old geezer. But Cooke's wealth, estimated to be somewhere in the neighborhood of $800 million, lets him live the kind of life most men in their eighties would have heart attacks just thinking about. In addition to all his other assets, from real estate to race horses, Cooke owns the Washington Redskins, and in the nation's capital that makes him one of the city's most potent sociopolitical sex symbols.

A much coveted seat in Cooke's private box at Redskins home games is the reward for sucking up to the onetime encyclopedia salesman. Political has-beens like George McGovern and Eugene McCarthy are regulars. So are assorted media personalities, such as columnist George Will, TV newswoman Lesley Stahl, and broadcaster Larry King. For special events, an occasional retired sports star often stops by. The late New York Yankee great Mickey Mantle once showed up to watch an old-timer's baseball game with a slinky brunette wearing a skintight T-shirt that read: "It tastes as good as it looks." Cooke was not present, but many of his friends who were got an eyeful.

"You gotta look at the front row—that's very important," King told *Vanity Fair.* "McGovern, McCarthy—they're not front-row guys. Now, I've been in the front with George Will and Dan Quayle, special invited guys. I'm usually six or seven down from Jack." In Washington, that's status.

Cooke's box has a tougher admissions policy than the Oval Office. Asked by a reporter if he planned on inviting President Bill Clinton to see a Redskins game, Cooke, with uncharacteristic brevity, replied, "No." Then after a moment's reflection he said, "Well, he *is* the President, so I suppose I will invite him if he calls and asks me."

The last woman to sit next to Cooke on a regular basis at RFK Stadium was Bolivian beauty Marlene Chalmers, wife number four and titular mistress of Cooke's horse farm in Middleburg, Virginia. That is, until she was arrested one night in 1993 for speeding through Georgetown with a young man she identified as her "nephew" riding on the hood of her Jaguar. A few months afterward, Cooke had the marriage annulled, and Chalmers was sent away with nothing.

Cooke's first wife, Jeannie, made out considerably better. In 1977, she was awarded the record sum of $42 million, one million dollars for every year she was married to her tycoon husband. Presiding judge Joseph A. Wapner, who later starred on TV's *People's Court,* figured the first Mrs. Cooke had earned it. She had visible tremors, a psychiatric report concluded, "and became so depressed that she attempted suicide four times."

In 1980, Cooke married his second wife, Jeanne Wilson, a Las Vegas sculptor. That marriage also ended in a bitter divorce. But not all of Cooke's ex-wives look back in anger.

"He was my mentor," Suzanne Martin, Cooke's third wife,

told Kitty Kelley. "He's probably the only father I never had."

Cooke married Suzanne in 1987, then divorced her seventy-three days later after she refused to have an abortion. Friends say he saw the pregnancy as a scheme to tap into his millions.

Before the marriage, Suzanne claimed that Cooke had forced her to have two abortions. She even hired the late trial attorney Edward Bennett Williams to sue her geriatric lover for $2 million. Williams, defender of Lucky Luciano and Jimmy Hoffa, and previously Cooke's own business partner, jumped at the chance, as he put it, "to flush that piece of shit out of this city once and for all." Martin dropped the suit when the little country squire finally promised to tie the knot.

Like Suzanne, Cooke's last wife, Marlene, is a convicted drug offender. Cooke, who insists that his football players and coaches set a moral example for Washington sports fans, seems to have developed a distinct taste in his golden years for female excons. When he met Marlene, she had already served time in a federal women's prison for conspiracy to import cocaine.

Suzanne and Marlene used to be friends, although Marlene was the smart one. So close were the two at one point that Suzanne loaned Marlene money for a postpenal tummy tuck. However, the friendship came to an abrupt end when Cooke's divorce from Suzanne made him a bachelor again and he and Marlene began dating.

In a city where politicians come and go, Cooke, who suffers from chronic claustrophobia, has been a continuing presence since 1979, the year he moved to Washington from Los Angeles to assume hands-on control of the football team he's called "the best hobby a man can have."

That hobby turned briefly troublesome when Cooke's former chauffeur, in an interview with a Washington magazine, claimed his boss told him that NFL games could be fixed. Cooke, denying these charges, sued the magazine, which settled out of court after the chauffeur informed lawyers he was once abducted by outer-space aliens.

Cooke had his own alien adventure in 1990, when he married Marlene, who at the time was thought to be divorced from Texas oilman David Chalmers. The new Mr. and Mrs. Cooke were an odd couple right from the start, seemingly living two separate lives, except during Redskins home games, when they showed up together in the owner's box.

First, Marlene mysteriously shot herself in the hand. Then, after months of talk that the marriage was on the rocks, she was arrested for drunk driving. Shortly afterward, Cooke announced that his wife's Dominican divorce "was falsely obtained" and therefore the two were "not legally married and never have been."

Marlene was still in prison when her divorce decree was issued, making the document null and void under Dominican law. That oversight allowed Cooke, as he put it, to return to "the life I lived before my purported marriage."

Marlene, though, wasn't that easy to get rid of. The U.S. Immigration and Naturalization Service has been trying to deport her back to South America for years with no success, thanks in large part to her attorney, Robert Bennett, who numbers Bill Clinton among his clients. According to her lawyers, Marlene provided the government with enough information to prosecute more than thirty "high-level narcotics traffickers" and should be allowed to stay in the United States, not "tossed in a trash can."

His ex-wife's plight must have moved the normally tight-fisted Cooke to take pity on her. Within weeks of announcing they were no longer married, he was apparently not only paying her legal bills but calling her his wife again. When the *New York Times* threw a reception on the eve of the 1994 Gridiron Club dinner, who should show up holding hands but Cooke and Marlene, now going by "Ramallo," one of the many last names from her romantic past. It hardly mattered what they called each other. Washington's most unpredictable May-December couple were an item again.

Had Cooke, who dumped more wives than most men can afford, mellowed in his old age? Or had he just succumbed to what the *Times* called the "dangerous glamour" of an inside-the-Beltway spider woman?

Apparently, neither. In Washington, where exotic babes can be hard to find, Cooke just wanted Marlene in his box during football season. And to make sure she'd be there, he married her. "Love is lovelier the second time around," Cooke said. "And that's the way it is with us."

Jack Kent Cooke (center) dines with archenemy Edward Bennett Williams, who once vowed to "flush" him out of town. Redskins general manager Bobby Betherd (left) looks on in amazement. *[Copyright Washington Post; reprinted by permission of the D.C. Public Library]*

Mrs. Jack Kent Cooke number four, the former Marlene Ramallo Chalmers, entertains the press after appearing in court on drunk-driving charges. *[Bill Thomas]*

18

"Bitch Set Me Up"

Few politicians in the nation's capital have been as relentlessly pursued by the press—and the police—as the mayor of Washington, Marion Barry. Originally elected in 1980, Barry's first three terms in office have been called the "longest striptease act" in city history. With aides and assistants going to jail on a regular basis, Barry somehow avoided a similar fate for ten years until his luck finally ran out.

Before he was arrested on a cocaine possession charge in 1990, rumors of Barry's drug use were common. One of his many ex-girlfriends was convicted of selling crack; a long-time associate was picked up in a narcotics raid; and Barry himself had to be rushed to the hospital after a suspected overdose at the 1987 Super Bowl.

Playing cat and mouse with the authorities seemed to be a hobby for Barry, who talked himself out of one embarrassing situation after another. The amazing thing was that most Washington voters believed him. When he was caught late at night hanging around the home of a stripper he'd seen at a local nightclub, he explained that he just wanted to meet her three-year-old son. Another time, Barry, a self-described "night owl," took an out-of-town reporter on a nocturnal tour of his favorite hangouts, boasting that he was too smart to get caught doing anything he shouldn't be doing.

An FBI videotape of Barry smoking crack in Washington's Vista International Hotel proved he wasn't. Lured to room 727 by a former girlfriend and onetime self-esteem instructor Hazel "Rasheeda" Moore, Barry was caught in the act.

"So what are you doing tonight?" Moore is heard asking on the tape.

"I hadn't planned too much. Why?" Barry replies. "What you got in mind?"

After the conversation turned to smoking crack, Barry wanted to know if Moore had a pipe. One was produced, the mayor lit up, and following his second puff, police and FBI agents stormed into the room.

"Goddamn, it was a fucking setup," Barry said as he was read his rights. "Bitch set me up."

Complaints from supporters that the mayor had been entrapped divided the city on the question of police tactics. Although Barry faced a long list of charges, a racially mixed jury found him guilty of only one: using a controlled substance. The judge wasn't so lenient and sentenced Barry to six months in a Virginia minimum-security prison, a harsh punishment for a first-time offender. Yet Barry, with the help of friends on the outside, managed to make the most of it. Two months into his sentence, prison officials at the federal penitentiary in Petersburg, Virginia, announced they were investigating reports that a female visitor had performed oral sex on Barry as dozens of inmates and their families looked on.

"You couldn't miss it. It was blatant, right in front of everybody," said Floyd Robertson, the prisoner who reported the incident to authorities. "I was trying not even to look, it was so disgusting," said Robertson's wife, who was sitting with her children several feet away from Barry. "It ruined our visit to have to witness that."

Barry, who denied the charge, did confess on *The Sally Jessy Raphael Show* that he had an uncontrollable appetite for sex. "It is part of [my] addiction," said Barry, at the time being treated for chemical dependency at a clinic in Florida. "This disease is cunning, baffling, powerful. It destroys your judgment."

Giving the same subject a racial twist, Barry told another talk-show host that the police, who arrested him, took unfair advantage of his weakness for sexy black women.

"If you notice, in this whole operation, it has been the FBI's strategy to use black women [as] bait," he said. "Most of us men have a great fondness in general for people of the opposite sex."

A prison commission found Barry guilty of the sex charge and transferred him to a medium-security penitentiary in Pennsylvania to serve out the balance of his sentence. Maybe the first of Barry's three wives had him figured out. "I'm just going to blow his dick off," Mary Treadwell said of her unfaithful husband. "It will save us all a lot of trouble."

After his release from jail, Barry announced that he had undergone a spiritual transformation while incarcerated. "The God force entered my mind" is the way he explained it to a group of supporters. Following his return to Washington, Barry changed his name to "Anwar Amal," donned African robes, and won a seat on the city council.

Recalling the amazing bounce-back ability of Boston mayor and congressman James M. Curley, Barry made his own comeback complete when he was elected mayor of Washington in 1994. One of his campaign promises was to rid the city of crime and drugs.

Friends say Barry's new wife, Cora, will make him toe the line. But who's keeping an eye on her? In 1987, the last time Barry was mayor, he had to ask for her resignation as the city's boxing and wrestling commissioner for double-billing more than $25,000 in expenses.

After leaving prison, where he received oral sex from a female visitor, Washington mayor Marion Barry told D.C. voters he had found God. *[Bill Thomas]*

Barry and D.C. delegate Eleanor Holmes Norton, who once owed the city $80,000 in unpaid taxes, appear on Capitol Hill to ask Congress for more money. *[Roll Call]*

19

Pack the Ripper

If power is the "ultimate aphrodisiac," as Henry Kissinger proposed, it didn't work for former Oregon senator Robert Packwood, who for more than twenty years led a double life as Washington's most unsuccessful Don Juan.

During his 1992 reelection campaign, Packwood was the subject of a story then being prepared by reporters at the *Washington Post.* When the article was finally published three weeks after the election, which Packwood won, it contained allegations by dozens of female aides, lobbyists, and campaign workers that the senator had made "unwanted sexual advances," grabbing, feeling, and kissing them in a sustained demonstration of unrequited passion dating all the way back to 1969.

One woman said that during an interview for a position on his campaign staff, Packwood, without asking permission, had chased her around his desk. Another reported that Packwood had attempted to massage her leg. And another said that Packwood, who was married for most of the time in question, told her: "If I ever run for president, I want you by my side as my vice-presidential running mate." The senator then "laid a juicy kiss on my lips, [and] I could feel his tongue coming," the woman said.

The *Post* article portrayed Packwood as a man so chronically unlucky at romance that he was reduced to standing on women's feet to keep them from running away, or else cornering them in his Senate office, where he kept a mood-enhancing selection of booze with which to ply his would-be dates. Despite his best efforts, Packwood apparently never scored with any of the women he pursued.

On paper, at least, Packwood was committed to a strict policy of hands off. In 1991, he and fifty-seven other senators signed a petition calling for members of Congress to refrain from "unwelcome flirtations," "ill-conceived dirty jokes," and other forms of male behavior defined as sexual harassment.

Packwood and two other signers, former senator Brock Adams and Sen. Daniel Inouye, were later accused, but never formally charged, of sexually harassing several different women: Adams for molesting eight women, allegedly using drugs to put some of them to sleep first, and Inouye for harassing a Honolulu hairdresser. Both Adams and Inouye denied the allegations, but Adams decided not to seek reelection.

It was Packwood who got all the attention, especially after it was revealed that his 8,200-page diary could contain information helpful to Democrats trying to drive him out of the Senate. Determined to keep his writings secret, Packwood let fellow lawmakers and the media know exactly what kind of tidbits he'd been saving for the last quarter century: "My lawyer put out a statement indicating some of the things that were in the diary, including an extended affair that one senator had with a member of his staff and an affair that a staffer had with a member of the current congressional Democratic leadership. . . . I want to emphasize . . . I have no intention of using this for blackmail, gray mail or anything else. I just want the Senate to clearly understand what it is the Ethics Committee has demanded. . . ."

By the time the full Senate met to decide what to do about the diaries, Packwood had already been typecast as a serial sex fiend. Female senators played a large part in the process, fanning the anti-Packwood fires for months to raise campaign funds. Sen. Barbara Boxer, a Democrat from California appointed to preside over a portion of the diary debates, was one of Packwood's most unrelenting foes, comparing him to Supreme Court Justice Clarence Thomas, the love-starved conservative whose futile attempts to turn on law professor Anita Hill made *Long Dong Silver* the most talked-about porno movie in America.

Demonstrating an almost otherworldly weirdness as the crisis escalated, Packwood took the Senate floor in his own defense, telling colleagues the story of how one of his female accusers had recently come to his office to apologize. She "put her arms around me, gave me a big kiss and said, 'You're wonderful.' "

It was a creepy yet touching moment. At this point, though, to concede Packwood was anything but a complete pervert—and an obstructionist pervert at that—would have been political suicide. By late 1995, in the face of charges that he had used his influence to get his ex-wife a job with a Washington lobbying firm, Packwood resigned from the Senate.

Not all Democrats joined the Packwood assault. Ted Kennedy, who had remained noticeably quiet during the Clarence Thomas hearings, had nothing to say. And neither did Democratic senator Chuck Robb of Virginia, who was dealing with a sex scandal of his own.

In a 1990 memo, Robb's then–press secretary tried to warn

his boss that stories circulating about his behavior "raised questions" concerning his judgment and credibility. The memo, entitled "Womanizing," went on to point out that despite Robb's denials it was well known that he had engaged in "oral sex . . . with at least a half-dozen women."

A few years earlier, Robb himself deftly addressed the oral-sex question in this carefully crafted memo: "I have to acknowledge that I have a weakness for the fairer sex," he wrote, "and I hope I never lose it. . . . But I have always drawn the line on certain conduct [despite being around] some very alluring company. . . . I haven't done anything that I regard as unfaithful to my wife, the only woman I [have] had coital sex with in the 20 years we've been married."

Robb admitted receiving a nude massage from an ex–beauty queen in New York, but steadfastly maintained that the rubdown was purely therapeutic. "First Clinton didn't inhale," went one joke around Washington, "then Robb didn't insert."

After reporters got hold of the memos, Robb was forced to respond, which he did in a letter to Virginia Democrats just prior to announcing his 1994 reelection bid against Iran-contra defendant and fellow ex-marine Oliver North.

"I'm vulnerable on the question of socializing under circumstances not appropriate for a married man," he declared, and then suggested that since his wife, Lynda Bird Johnson Robb, had forgiven him, so should voters, assuming not too many of them linked "socializing" to oral sex, a crime punishable under Virginia's sodomy laws by twenty years in prison.

The explanation must have worked. Chuck Robb was reelected.

Sen. Robert Packwood, who plied his female prey with cheap wine, poses in front of his office liquor collection. *[Roll Call]*

Some of the women accusing Packwood of sexual harassment hold a press conference to discuss his technique. Rep. Pat Schroeder (right) gives moral support. *[Roll Call]*

After receiving a nude rubdown from an ex–beauty queen, Sen. Chuck Robb gives his wife, Lynda Bird, a neck massage. *[Roll Call]*

20

Dogpatch
on the Potomac

The sexual and financial accusations that followed Bill and Hillary Clinton from Arkansas to Washington made them the most controversial twosome to occupy the White House since the Roosevelts.

It's safe to say that no sitting president this century has been bombarded by the kind of character attacks that have been aimed at Clinton. Before the 1992 primaries, a nightclub singer named Gennifer Flowers accused him of having a twelve-year affair with her. The charges were so believable to many that both Clintons appeared on *60 Minutes* to answer them. Clinton denied having the affair but did admit causing unspecified "pain" in his marriage.

He repeated the same theme later on *The Phil Donahue Show.* "I've told you the only facts I think you're entitled to know," Clinton said. "Have I had any problems with my marriage? Yes. Are we in good shape now? Yes."

Breaking with a tradition established by other political girlfriends, Flowers later appeared nude not in *Playboy* but in *Penthouse.* Just in time for the election, the issue pictured her in a dozen provocative poses. There was also a lengthy interview in which she described Clinton's lovemaking technique in graphic detail.

"We made love everywhere: on the floor, in bed, in the kitchen, on the cabinet and on the sink," she said, rating Clinton a "9" out of a possible "10" as a lover. "He ate pussy like a champ," she told *Penthouse.* "I'd have to say, 'Whoa, boy, come on up here.' He was so aggressive with that." In a dig at the First Lady, Flowers went on to say, "I dare Hillary to bare her butt in any magazine. They don't have a page that broad."

Conservatives in Congress tried without success to turn the *Penthouse* article into an election-eve bombshell, but voters seemed no longer interested in Flowers or her charges.

Rumors about Clinton's extramarital relations never hurt his reputation in Arkansas. In Washington, though, that would all change. By the end of Clinton's first year in office, several Arkansas state troopers, who once served as bodyguards for the former governor, came forward with information that seemed to corroborate stories told by Flowers and others about Clinton's Little Rock sex life.

In what would become known as "Troopergate," the police officers spoke to reporters about how they had helped to facilitate meetings between Clinton and a series of regular girlfriends, including Flowers, whose skill at giving oral sex Clinton once praised by telling a state trooper that she "could suck a tennis ball through a garden hose."

One trooper detailed Clinton's romantic rendezvous with a Little Rock woman, who drove to the governor's mansion late one night in a pickup truck. "The governor came out of the residence and climbed in the front seat of the truck, which was parked in an area near the drive," said Trooper Larry Patterson, who watched the action unfold on TV monitors in the police guardhouse. Focusing security cameras on the truck, which the woman had driven to a back parking lot, Patterson said he pointed the camera "directly into the windshield, and watched on the screen" as the governor received oral sex.

The list of alleged Clinton mistresses is long and varied. A former Miss Arkansas claimed to have had an affair with Clinton in 1983. The woman also said she was threatened with violence by a Democratic Party official for telling her story to the press. A reputed prostitute claimed that she and Clinton had thirteen encounters and that she had given birth to his child. At least fifteen other women, ranging from a prominent judge to a cosmetics store clerk, all say they have had sex with Clinton.

By far, the most politically troublesome of the so-called "bimbo eruptions" involved Paula Jones, an Arkansas state employee when, she claims, Clinton attempted to have sex with her in a hotel room. Jones charged in a $700,000 lawsuit against the president that Clinton, while he was governor, lured her into a room at Little Rock's Excelsior Hotel for what she thought was a job interview.

After being summoned by a state trooper to meet with Clinton during an economic development conference, Jones entered the governor's hotel room. "Clinton then took Jones's hand and pulled her toward him," her suit claims. "[He] put his hand on [Jones's] leg and started sliding it toward the hem of [her] culottes. . . . Jones exclaimed 'What are you doing?' and escaped from Clinton's physical proximity by walking away from him. [She later took a seat at the end of the sofa nearest the door.] . . . Clinton asked [her] 'Are you married?' She responded that she had a regular boyfriend. Clinton then approached the sofa and as he sat down he lowered his trousers and underwear exposing his erect penis and asked Jones to 'kiss it.' " The suit then notes that "there are distinguishing characteristics in Clinton's genital area that were obvious to Jones."

As Clinton tried to put his arm around her, Jones jumped up and said, "Look, I have to go." Then, according to the suit, "Clinton, while fondling his penis said, 'Well, I don't want to make you do anything you don't want to do.'

"As Jones left the room, Clinton looked sternly at [her] and said, 'You are smart. Let's keep this between ourselves.' "

Jones, who was attacked by most feminist groups, was defended by Anita Hill, probably the most famous victim of sexual harassment. Even people "we admire and respect and want to do well may engage in behavior that is objectionable," Hill said, referring to Clinton.

Many conservatives also supported Jones, whose good-girl image was tarnished in late 1994, when *Penthouse* published topless pictures of her taken by an old boyfriend. An accompanying article described her as "someone dedicated to snaring men who could buy her clothes and nights on the town she couldn't afford."

Meanwhile, an Arkansas judge in the case said that no trial could begin until the president leaves office. Nevertheless, pretrial discovery could proceed, which allowed lawyers to gather depositions and affidavits from all witnesses, even Bill Clinton. Jones asked the court for permission to submit as evidence a drawing of the president's penis.

Hillary Clinton, who was aware of her husband's escapades, apparently had her own reasons to appreciate his frequent trips out of Arkansas. The troopers told *The American Spectator* magazine that they suspected Hillary was having an affair with Vince Foster, a partner in the Rose law firm where she worked and one of her husband's closest friends. Some of the troopers said they performed approximately the same duties for Hillary as they did for Clinton, driving her and Foster to a mountain retreat outside of Little Rock, where the two spent "significant amounts of time alone."

After Clinton was elected president, Foster became a White House counsel. One of his duties involved keeping a lid on the Clintons' Arkansas investment portfolio, with particular emphasis on their involvement in Whitewater, a resort property in the Ozarks they purchased together with James McDougal, president of Madison Savings and Loan in Little Rock.

Several months prior to a federal investigation of Madison, Foster shot himself to death in a park along the Potomac River on July 20, 1993. A special prosecutor could find no connection between his death and the Whitewater-Madison case, but circumstances surrounding the incident continue to raise questions about what Foster knew.

The night before his suicide, Foster was invited by Clinton to watch a movie with him. Foster declined, saying he had too much work to do. Later, in a deposition, Clinton said he had no idea his friend was busy at the time preparing three years' worth of overdue income tax returns for the Whitewater Development Corporation, the First Family's mysterious business venture.

Bill Clinton busts a gut at his White House birthday party, as elected officials and wife, Hillary, cheer him on. *[Roll Call]*

Gennifer Flowers, one of Clinton's many ex-girlfriends, says he called her breasts "the girls." *[Bill Thomas]*

PHONE FREAK

Rep. Mel Reynolds seemed destined for political success. In 1992, the black, Oxford-educated freshman was
named to the House Ways and Means Committee, a rare
honor for anyone, let alone a congressional rookie. But
it didn't take long for Reynolds, married and the father
of three children, to get into trouble. In 1994, the same
year his mentor, Ways and Means chairman Dan Rostenkowski, was indicted on numerous counts of defrauding
the U.S. Government and witness tampering, Reynolds,
a Chicago Democrat, was accused of having sex with a
female minor, soliciting child pornography and obstructing justice.

In court a year later, Reynolds denied the charges, but
admitted having an embarrassing weakness for "phone
sex." His chief accuser, Beverly Heard, was sixteen
when she and Reynolds first met, and police tapes of
their conversations provided key evidence in the case
against him.

In one tape Reynolds and Heard talk about an upcom-
ing date:

MEL: What you gonna wear?
BEVERLY: Well, my peach underwear, like you told me
to. I was hoping that we could do something really
special . . .
MEL: I was definitely gonna stick my dick in you.
BEVERLY: Really?
MEL: Right in my office . . .
BEVERLY: Really?
MEL: I was looking forward to it.

In the same conversation, Heard and Reynolds relive
some of their old times together:

150

BEVERLY: Remember what you used to call me?
MEL: What was that?
BEVERLY: Sweet Young Pussy.
MEL: What?
BEVERLY: Sweet Young—
MEL: Sweet, Young Pussy.
BEVERLY: You don't remember that?
MEL: It was definitely sweet—
BEVERLY: Cause I was 16 . . .
MEL: And young.
BEVERLY: Yeah.
MEL: Yeah, buddy . . .

Later, Heard introduces "Theresa," a fictitious 15-year-old girl Reynolds is anxious to meet.

MEL: Where does she go to school?
BEVERLY: Uh, she said, uhm, oh goodness, I think it's Our Lady of Peace, something like that.
MEL: Lady of Peace. A Catholic school.

Telephone tapes helped to convict Rhodes Scholar Rep. Mel Reynolds of having sex with a teenage girl in Chicago. *[Roll Call]*

BEVERLY: Huh? Yes.
MEL: Jesus, a Catholic—
BEVERLY: A Catholic school girl . . .
MEL: Did I win the Lotto?

Testifying in court, Reynolds said he didn't "have any idea" what he meant by that last comment. "It's a really nutty thing," he said. "I don't even play the Lotto."

A jury in Chicago found him guilty on all charges. Reynolds was sentenced to five years in prison.

Postscript

"There's a 'For Sale' sign on the United States Capitol," said Sen. Tim Wirth shortly after he retired from active lawmaking in 1992. Freed from having to run for reelection, Wirth was also free to tell the truth.

What's amazing, though, is how relatively little it costs to buy into the kind of assistance Congress puts on sale every day. A few thousand dollars here, a few thousand more there, and before too long it's possible to have your own congressional caucus on retainer.

That's how the insurance industry thought of the powerful House Ways and Means Committee in 1990, when its lobbyists rendezvoused with committee members for a week's worth of fun in Barbados. With transportation to and from the resort island provided at taxpayer expense, lawmakers and their spouses enjoyed golf, tennis, and other activities remotely connected to legislative work, while influence peddlers picked up the tab.

All of this would have been business as usual if ABC News hadn't captured the good times on videotape for showing on national television. Four Ways and Means members—Marty Russo, Thomas Downey, Ray McGrath, and Guy Vander Jagt—can thank the resulting bad publicity for ending their long careers on the Hill. But before you think corruption is on the run in Washington, consider that in 1992, Russo, Downey, McGrath, and Vander Jagt, plus thirty-two other departing members of Congress, all stayed in town to become lobbyists themselves.

Refusing to see his loss at the polls as a personal defeat, maybe Vander Jagt put it best. "I like to point out that the fellow who beat me tripled both of our salaries," he said.

Today's scandal is tomorrow's career opportunity.

In what could be Washington's first suicide memo, Vincent Foster, the late White House lawyer, wrote that in Washington "ruining people is considered sport." The poor guy had it all wrong. It's *serious* business. Nevertheless, not everyone touched by scandal ends up being ruined. Some, in fact, like Richard Nixon, Gary Hart, Barney Frank, and Marion Barry, rebounded quite nicely.

Teapot Dome, Watergate, ABSCAM, and Monkey Business may be code names for high-level sleaze. But they're also reminders of how amusing a pastime following politics can really be. Which is why, as we get ready to close the book on twentieth-century Washington, it's only natural to wonder what the future holds.

Will sex and money continue to lure politicians and their pals into embarrassing situations? Will reformers rant and pundits rave? Will the next century in the nation's capital be as full of scandalous behavior as this one has been?

Let's hope so.

Richard Nixon pays his final visit to Congress in 1992. *[Roll Call]*

BILL THOMAS, a former reporter for the Baltimore *Sun*, began his career as a journalist at *Congressional Quarterly*. He is the former editor of *Dossier* magazine and the *Washington Weekly*. He has been a commentator for National Public Radio and has written for numerous publications, including *Vanity Fair, Spy, The Washington Post,* and the *Los Angeles Times Magazine*. Thomas is the author ot *Club Fed*, and the coauthor of *Lawyers and Thieves* and *Red Tape: Adventure Capitalism in the New Russia*. Currently, he is a contributing editor to the Capitol Hill paper *Roll Call*.